MEDITERRANEAN DIET Cookbook for Beginners

YOUR STEP-BY-STEP GUIDE TO HEALTHY EATING AND LASTING WEIGHT LOSS. INCLUDES 100 FULL-COLOR RECIPES AND A 28-DAY PLAN

Gertraud Kron

Table of Content

Chapter 1: Introduction to the Mediterranean Diet

1.1 Welcome to the Mediterranean Lifestyle

The Mediterranean diet isn't just a diet—it's a comprehensive lifestyle rooted in the culinary traditions of the countries bordering the Mediterranean Sea, such as Italy, Greece, Spain, and Morocco. This diet is celebrated worldwide for its rich flavors and profound health benefits. It encapsulates a way of eating that is both balanced and sustainable, emphasizing enjoyment of food, life, and social dining.

1.2 Understanding the Mediterranean Diet

The Mediterranean diet focuses on the consumption of natural, whole foods. Central to this diet are:

- **Vegetables and fruits:** Consumed in abundance at every meal.
- **Whole grains:** Integral to daily eating.
- **Healthy fats:** Predominantly sourced from olive oil.
- **Lean proteins:** Mainly from plant sources, fish, and seafood. This diet minimizes the intake of processed foods, sugars, and red meats, distinguishing it from many Western dietary patterns.

1.3 Historical and Cultural Origins

The Mediterranean diet has evolved over millennia, influenced by the geographical, economic, and cultural landscapes of the Mediterranean region. This diet was first popularized in the 1950s following studies that showed lower rates of chronic disease and higher life expectancy among populations in the Mediterranean area compared to other Western countries.

1.4 Scientific Backing and Health Benefits

Numerous studies have highlighted the Mediterranean diet's benefits, which include:

- **Heart Health:** Reduced risk of heart disease, thanks to a high intake of heart-healthy fats from olive oil and nuts.
- **Weight Management:** Natural portion control through high fiber intake from whole grains and vegetables.
- **Diabetes Prevention:** Improved blood sugar levels from a diet low in refined sugars and high in dietary fiber.
- **Cancer Prevention:** Antioxidants from fruits and vegetables help in reducing cancer risk.
- **Cognitive Benefits:** There's emerging evidence that this diet may also enhance cognitive function and reduce the risk of Alzheimer's disease.

1.5 Key Principles of the Mediterranean Diet

Adopting the Mediterranean diet involves more than just changing the food you eat. It also includes:

- **Eating with Others:** Meals are often social occasions.
- **Seasonal and Fresh Foods:** Emphasizes foods that are in season and locally sourced.
- **Physical Activity:** Regular physical activity is an integral part of the lifestyle.

1.6 Why This Cookbook?

This cookbook is designed to ease you into the Mediterranean way of eating by providing simple, delicious recipes that can be made with readily available ingredients. It's crafted to help beginners understand the principles of the diet, learn how to prepare the dishes that embody it, and integrate these eating habits into a comprehensive lifestyle change.

Chapter 2: What is the Mediterranean Diet?

2.1 Overview of the Diet

The Mediterranean diet is based on the traditional eating habits of the people living in countries bordering the Mediterranean Sea. It is not a single prescriptive diet but rather a flexible eating pattern. At its heart, it involves a high intake of vegetables, fruits, whole grains, legumes, and nuts; moderate consumption of fish, poultry, and dairy products; and minimal consumption of red meat.

2.2 Core Foods of the Mediterranean Diet

The Mediterranean diet is celebrated for its variety and emphasis on whole, unprocessed foods. Below is a detailed look at the core foods integral to this eating pattern:

Vegetables and Fruits

- **Role in the Diet:** Vegetables and fruits are the cornerstone of the Mediterranean diet, consumed in abundance at every meal. They are vital sources of vitamins, minerals, fiber, and antioxidants.
- **Typical Varieties:** Includes leafy greens (spinach, kale), Mediterranean staples like tomatoes, cucumbers, and bell peppers, and fruits such as figs, grapes, and citrus.
- **Preparation Tips:** Vegetables can be enjoyed raw in salads, roasted to enhance their flavor, or cooked into stews and sauces. Fruits are often eaten fresh as snacks or desserts.

Whole Grains

- **Role in the Diet:** Whole grains provide essential nutrients and dietary fiber, which help in digestion and prolong satiety.
- **Typical Varieties:** Commonly consumed grains include whole wheat, oats, brown rice, barley, and farro.
- **Preparation Tips:** Grains are often used as bases for salads, side dishes, or integral parts of main dishes, like in tabbouleh or risotto.

Legumes and Nuts

- **Role in the Diet:** These are important for their high protein content, healthy fats, and fibers. They also serve as a great meat substitute for vegetarian dishes.
- **Typical Varieties:** Includes beans, lentils, chickpeas, almonds, walnuts, and pistachios.
- **Preparation Tips:** Legumes can be turned into dips (like hummus), added to soups and salads, or served as a main dish. Nuts are great as snacks or added to dishes for extra texture and flavor.

Healthy Fats

- **Role in the Diet:** Healthy fats are a central part of the diet, particularly from olive oil, which is used generously in cooking and as a dressing.
- **Typical Varieties:** Extra virgin olive oil is the most prized for its flavor and nutritional profile. Other healthy fats include avocados and seeds (like sesame and sunflower).
- **Preparation Tips:** Use olive oil for sautéing or as a base for dressings. Avocados can be eaten alone, in salads, or mashed as spreads.

Herbs and Spices

- **Role in the Diet:** Herbs and spices are used extensively to enhance flavor without the need for salt, contributing to the diet's health benefits.
- **Typical Varieties:** Includes garlic, basil, mint, rosemary, sage, cinnamon, and pepper.
- **Preparation Tips:** Fresh herbs are often sprinkled over dishes before serving to preserve their flavors and health benefits. Dried herbs and spices are used during cooking to infuse dishes with robust flavors.

Protein Sources

- **Fish and Seafood:** High in protein and omega-3 fatty acids, recommended to be consumed several times a week.
- **Poultry and Eggs:** Eaten in moderation, they provide high-quality protein.
- **Dairy:** Fermented dairy products like yogurt and cheese are consumed in moderate amounts, mainly as condiments or desserts.
- **Red Meat:** Limited to a few times a month to minimize intake of saturated fats.

Wine

- **Role in the Diet:** Wine, especially red, is consumed in moderation and typically with meals. It's considered to have heart-health benefits when consumed responsibly.
- **Preparation Tips:** Wine is meant to complement the flavors of meals and enhance the dining experience, not to be used as a primary beverage throughout the day.

Understanding these core foods and how to incorporate them into your daily meals is crucial for adopting the Mediterranean diet. This guide not only provides a foundation for healthy eating but also invites creativity and variety in the kitchen.

2.3 Dietary Practices

- **Moderate Wine Consumption:** Wine, particularly red, is consumed regularly but moderately with meals. It is considered to have beneficial effects when taken in moderation.
- **Water as the Main Beverage:** Water is the main drink of choice, with coffee and tea being acceptable without added sugars.
- **Mindful Eating:** Meals are eaten slowly, savoring every bite, which helps in portion control and full digestion.

2.4 Benefits of the Mediterranean Diet

- **Cardiovascular Health:** The diet has been shown to significantly reduce the risk of developing heart disease, thanks to its emphasis on heart-healthy fats and high fiber.
- **Prevention of Metabolic Syndrome and Diabetes:** It helps in regulating blood sugar and improving insulin sensitivity.
- **Weight Loss and Management:** High in fiber and healthy fats, it helps in maintaining a healthy weight without the need to count calories.
- **Mental Health:** Some studies suggest a correlation between the Mediterranean diet and a lower risk of depression, along with improved cognitive function.

2.5 Cultural Significance and Sustainability

The Mediterranean diet is deeply woven into the cultural fabric of the regions from which it originates. It promotes not only a balanced diet but also sustainable food practices, such as seasonal eating and supporting local agriculture, which have minimal environmental impact compared to other dietary patterns.

2.6 Getting Started with the Mediterranean Diet

This section would introduce practical tips on how to start integrating the Mediterranean diet into daily life, such as:

- **Stocking the Mediterranean Pantry:** A guide to essential ingredients to keep on hand.
- **Simple Swaps for Daily Eating:** Suggestions for replacing common staples with Mediterranean alternatives.
- **Incorporating More Vegetables and Fruits:** Tips for increasing daily intake.

Chapter 3: Introduction to the Causes and Types of the Mediterranean Diet

3.1 Geographical Influences

The Mediterranean Sea touches the shores of Europe, Asia, and Africa, with each region bringing its unique flavors and culinary practices to the diet. This diversity is why there isn't a single "Mediterranean diet" but rather a spectrum of eating styles among the countries in the Mediterranean basin.

- **Southern Europe:** Countries like Italy, Greece, and Spain emphasize olive oil, pasta, fish, and legumes.
- **Middle East and North Africa:** Nations such as Morocco, Lebanon, and Turkey favor lamb, yogurt, and a variety of spices like cumin and coriander.
- **Coastal Regions:** Areas close to the sea have a diet heavy in seafood, whereas inland regions might focus more on agricultural products like grains and dairy.

3.2 Cultural and Historical Causes

The development of the Mediterranean diet is deeply intertwined with the history and culture of the region. Historically, the diet was influenced by the agricultural resources available in a given area, trade between regions, and religious practices that dictated dietary restrictions.

- **Ancient Trade Routes:** The spread of ingredients like spices, grains, and fruits across the region was facilitated by trade among Mediterranean countries and with the rest of the world.
- **Religious Practices:** Dietary restrictions and fasting periods in religions such as Christianity, Islam, and Judaism have shaped food choices and meal timings in different parts of the Mediterranean.

3.3 Types of Mediterranean Diets

While there are common core elements, the Mediterranean diet can vary significantly from one area to another. This section introduces the main types, categorized by their regional characteristics.

- **Eastern Mediterranean:** Rich in olive oil, fruits, vegetables, nuts, and grains with a heavy emphasis on seafood.
- **Western Mediterranean:** Characterized by a high intake of dairy, particularly cheese and yogurt, alongside fruits, vegetables, and poultry.
- **Southern Mediterranean:** Often includes more legumes, root vegetables, and lamb, and uses specific spices that distinguish it from other regions.

3.4 Nutritional Variations

Each regional diet within the Mediterranean spectrum has its nutritional highlights, adapting to the local environment, available resources, and cultural preferences. This adaptability not only makes the Mediterranean diet versatile but also accessible to people worldwide, allowing them to adjust the diet based on local ingredients.

- **Nutrient Density:** Despite regional variations, the common thread is a focus on nutrient-dense foods that provide a variety of health benefits.
- **Adaptability:** The diet's flexibility encourages substitutions that can cater to regional tastes and seasonal availability, making it sustainable and enjoyable.

3.5 Implementing Regional Varieties

For beginners, understanding these regional varieties can help personalize the Mediterranean diet to fit individual preferences and available local produce. This section will provide guidance on how to incorporate different regional dishes into a balanced eating plan.

- **Recipe Adaptations:** Suggestions on how to modify classic recipes to fit the Mediterranean profile using local ingredients.
- **Seasonal Menus:** Example menus that reflect seasonal variations and demonstrate how to balance meals throughout the year.

Chapter 4: Benefits of the Mediterranean Diet

4.1 Heart Health

- **Reduced Risk of Heart Disease:** The Mediterranean diet is rich in heart-healthy fats from olive oil, nuts, and fish, which have been shown to lower bad cholesterol levels and reduce the risk of heart disease.
- **Blood Pressure Management:** Regular consumption of fruits, vegetables, and whole grains, all staples in the Mediterranean diet, helps to lower blood pressure naturally.

4.2 Weight Management

- **Natural Portion Control:** High fiber content from fruits, vegetables, and whole grains promotes a feeling of fullness, helping to reduce overall calorie intake without the need for calorie counting.
- **Sustainable Weight Loss:** Unlike restrictive diets, the Mediterranean diet offers a varied and enjoyable eating plan that is easier to maintain long-term.

4.3 Diabetes Prevention and Management

- **Blood Sugar Regulation:** The diet's low glycemic index foods help in stabilizing blood sugar levels.

- **Insulin Sensitivity Improvement:** Regular consumption of healthy fats and fibers improves insulin sensitivity, which can help prevent type 2 diabetes and manage the condition in those already diagnosed.

4.4 Cancer Prevention

- **Antioxidant-Rich Foods:** The abundance of fruits and vegetables provides antioxidants that protect cells from damage that can lead to cancer.
- **Anti-inflammatory Properties:** Chronic inflammation is a known risk factor for cancer, and the Mediterranean diet's focus on anti-inflammatory foods like leafy greens and tomatoes helps reduce this risk.

4.5 Bone Health

- **Calcium and Vitamin D:** Moderate consumption of dairy products, along with fish and sunlight exposure, provides calcium and vitamin D, essential for bone health.
- **Reduced Risk of Osteoporosis:** The diet's nutrient-dense foods support bone density and overall skeletal strength.

4.6 Improved Mental Health

- **Cognitive Function:** Diets rich in omega-3 fatty acids, as found in fish and nuts, have been linked to reduced rates of cognitive decline and dementia.
- **Mood Regulation:** The diet's balance of complex carbohydrates, essential fats, and proteins can stabilize blood sugar and hormone levels, which are crucial for mood regulation.

4.7 Longevity and Overall Well-Being

- **Life Expectancy:** People adhering to a Mediterranean diet have been shown to have a higher life expectancy, thanks in part to the diet's role in reducing the risk of developing chronic diseases.
- **Quality of Life:** The diet encourages a lifestyle that includes physical activity, social meals, and a balanced approach to life, all of which contribute to overall well-being.

4.8 Environmental Benefits

- **Sustainability:** The emphasis on plant-based foods and local sourcing supports sustainable farming practices, which are less taxing on the environment compared to diets high in processed foods and meat.

4.9 How to Maximize These Benefits

- **Practical Tips:** Tips for effectively integrating the Mediterranean diet into daily life, such as opting for whole over processed foods, incorporating more fruits and vegetables, and choosing healthy fats.
- **Personal Stories:** Testimonials and case studies from individuals who have experienced significant health improvements by adopting the Mediterranean diet.

Chapter 5: Shopping List, Foods to Eat, and Foods to Avoid

5.1 Building Your Mediterranean Pantry

- **Essentials to Stock Up On:** A comprehensive list of staples needed to follow the Mediterranean diet, including olive oil, whole grains, legumes, nuts, seeds, herbs, and spices.
- **Choosing the Right Products:** Tips on selecting high-quality products such as how to pick the best olive oil (extra virgin), the freshest produce, and sustainably sourced fish and seafood.

5.2 Foods to Eat

This section provides a detailed list of foods that are the cornerstone of the Mediterranean diet, organized by food groups:

- **Vegetables:** Emphasize a variety of all colors, such as leafy greens, tomatoes, broccoli, peppers, and eggplants. Aim for fresh, local, and seasonal but frozen can be a good alternative.
- **Fruits:** Focus on whole fruits like apples, oranges, berries, figs, peaches, and grapes. Prefer fresh or frozen without added sugars.
- **Whole Grains:** Include options like whole wheat, brown rice, barley, quinoa, and farro.
- **Proteins:**
    - **Legumes:** Beans, peas, lentils, and chickpeas.
    - **Nuts and Seeds:** Almonds, walnuts, flaxseeds, and pumpkin seeds.
    - **Seafood:** Salmon, mackerel, trout, and light canned tuna.
    - **Poultry:** Chicken and turkey.
    - **Dairy:** Greek yogurt, cheese, especially feta and Parmesan in moderation.
- **Herbs and Spices:** Basil, mint, rosemary, sage, cinnamon, nutmeg, and black pepper.
- **Fats:** Primarily from olive oil, but also from avocados and olives.

5.3 Foods to Avoid or Limit

Identify foods that are not typically part of the Mediterranean diet and suggest limiting their intake:

- **Red Meat:** Limit consumption to a few times per month and opt for lean cuts when consumed.
- **Processed Foods and Sugars:** Avoid or limit foods high in processed sugars and refined grains, such as sweets, soda, and white bread.
- **High-Fat Dairy Products:** Limit whole milk, cream, and butter.
- **Processed Meats:** Such as sausages, hot dogs, and deli meats.
- **Refined Oils and Fats:** Reduce intake of highly refined or hydrogenated oils like soybean oil, canola oil, and margarine.

5.4 Smart Shopping Tips

- **Planning Ahead:** Encourage readers to plan their meals for the week ahead and make a shopping list to avoid impulse buys.

- **Seasonal Buying:** Tips on buying seasonal produce for the best flavor and value.
- **Local and Organic Options:** Advantages of choosing local and organic products when available and affordable.

5.5 Sample Shopping List

Provide a sample shopping list that includes a variety of foods from the Mediterranean diet. This list can serve as a template for beginners when they go grocery shopping, ensuring they cover all nutritional bases.

In this introductory chapter, we warmly welcome you to your journey towards a kidney-friendly diet. By holding this book, you have already taken the first step towards actively supporting and improving your health. Being diagnosed with kidney disease or advised to follow a kidney-sparing diet can initially be overwhelming. However, worry not, as this cookbook will not only show you how to prepare tasty and healthy dishes but also explain why they

BREAKFAST

1. Toast with Guacamole and Fried Egg Yolk

★★★☆☆

🕐 5 Minutes   🍳🕐 5 Minutes   🍴 1 servings

INGREDIENTS

- 1 slice of whole grain bread
- 1 ripe avocado
- 1 egg
- 1 tablespoon lime juice
- Salt and pepper to taste
- A pinch of chili flakes (optional)
- Fresh cilantro for garnish

INSTRUCTIONS

1. Toast the bread to your desired level of crispiness using a toaster or oven.
2. Prepare the guacamole: In a small bowl, mash the ripe avocado with lime juice, salt, and pepper. You can add chili flakes for a bit of heat if desired.
3. Fry the egg: Heat a non-stick skillet over medium heat and carefully crack the egg into the pan, keeping the yolk intact. Fry until the edges are crispy and the yolk is still runny, about 3 minutes.
4. Assemble the toast: Spread the guacamole evenly over the toasted bread. Carefully place the fried egg on top.
5. Garnish and serve: Sprinkle fresh cilantro over the top and enjoy immediately.

Nutritional : Calories: 345 kcal | Protein: 11 g | Carbohydrates: 30 g | Fat: 21 g | Fiber: 9 g | Sugar: 3 g

2. Stacked Pancakes with Berries

★★★☆☆

🕐 10 Minutes   🍳🕐 15 Minutes   🍴 2 servings

INGREDIENTS

- 1 cup whole wheat flour
- 1 teaspoon baking powder
- 1 cup milk
- 1 egg
- 1 tablespoon honey
- 1/2 teaspoon vanilla extract
- 1 cup mixed berries (strawberries, blueberries, raspberries)
- Maple syrup (for serving)

INSTRUCTIONS

1. Combine the whole wheat flour and baking powder in a large mixing bowl.
2. In another bowl, whisk together the milk, egg, honey, and vanilla extract.
3. Pour the wet ingredients into the dry ingredients and stir until just combined.
4. Heat a non-stick skillet over medium heat and pour 1/4 cup of batter for each pancake. Cook until bubbles form on the surface, then flip and cook until golden brown on both sides.
5. Serve the pancakes stacked high with fresh berries on top and a drizzle of maple syrup.

Nutritional : Calories: 375 kcal | Protein: 12 g | Carbohydrates: 65 g | Fat: 8 g | Fiber: 8 g | Sugar: 18 g

INGREDIENTS

- 1 tablespoon olive oil
- 1 small onion, diced
- 1 bell pepper, diced
- 2 cloves garlic, minced
- 1 can (14 oz) diced tomatoes
- 1 teaspoon paprika
- 1/2 teaspoon cumin
- 4 eggs
- Salt and pepper to taste
- Fresh parsley for garnish

3. Shakshuka in a Frying Pan

★★★★★

5 Minutes   25 Minutes   2 servings

INSTRUCTIONS

1. Heat olive oil in a large frying pan over medium heat. Add the onion and bell pepper, and sauté until softened.
2. Add garlic and cook for another minute until fragrant.
3. Stir in the diced tomatoes, paprika, and cumin. Simmer the sauce for about 10 minutes until it thickens slightly.
4. Make four wells in the sauce and crack an egg into each well. Cover the pan and cook until the eggs are set to your liking.
5. Season with salt and pepper, garnish with fresh parsley, and serve hot.

Nutritional : Calories: 290 kcal | Protein: 16 g | Carbohydrates: 20 g | Fat: 17 g | Fiber: 4 g | Sugar: 10 g

INGREDIENTS

- 2 eggs
- 1/4 cup diced bell peppers
- 1/4 cup diced tomatoes
- 1/4 cup spinach, chopped
- 1 tablespoon olive oil
- Salt and pepper to taste
- 1 slice gluten-free bread, toasted

4. Scrambled Eggs with Vegetables and Gluten-Free Toast

★★★★★

5 Minutes   10 Minutes   1 servings

INSTRUCTIONS

1. Heat olive oil in a skillet over medium heat. Add the bell peppers and tomatoes, sautéing until they are soft.
2. Add the spinach and cook until wilted.
3. Beat the eggs in a bowl and pour them into the skillet. Stir gently until the eggs are fully cooked and scrambled.
4. Season with salt and pepper.
5. Serve the scrambled eggs with a side of toasted gluten-free bread.

Nutritional : Calories: 320 kcal | Protein: 18 g | Carbohydrates: 18 g | Fat: 20 g | Fiber: 3 g | Sugar: 5 g

5. Lemon Muffin

★★★★★

🕐 15 Minutes   🍳🕐 20 Minutes   🍴 6 servings

INGREDIENTS

- 2 cups almond flour
- 1/2 cup sugar
- 1 teaspoon baking powder
- 1/4 cup olive oil
- 2 eggs
- Juice and zest of 1 lemon
- 1/4 cup almond milk

INSTRUCTIONS

1. Preheat the oven to 350°F (175°C). Line a muffin tin with paper liners.
2. In a bowl, mix together the almond flour, sugar, and baking powder.
3. In another bowl, whisk the olive oil, eggs, lemon juice, lemon zest, and almond milk.
4. Combine the wet and dry ingredients and mix until smooth.
5. Divide the batter evenly among the muffin cups.
6. Bake for 20 minutes, or until a toothpick inserted into the center comes out clean.
7. Let cool before serving.

Nutritional : Calories: 275 kcal | Protein: 8 g | Carbohydrates: 20 g | Fat: 20 g | Fiber: 3 g | Sugar: 12 g

6. Spinach and Ricotta Omelette

★★★★★

🕐 5 Minutes   🍳🕐 10 Minutes   🍴 1 servings

INSTRUCTIONS

1. Beat the eggs in a bowl with salt and pepper.
2. Heat olive oil in a skillet over medium heat. Add the spinach and sauté until wilted.
3. Pour the beaten eggs over the spinach. Dollop the ricotta cheese across the surface of the egg as it cooks.
4. Cook until the eggs are set and the bottom is golden brown. Fold the omelette in half and serve hot.

INGREDIENTS

- 2 eggs
- 1/2 cup fresh spinach, chopped
- 1/4 cup ricotta cheese
- 1 tablespoon olive oil
- Salt and pepper to taste

Nutritional : Calories: 340 kcal | Protein: 21 g | Carbohydrates: 3 g | Fat: 27 g | Fiber: 1 g | Sugar: 2 g

7. Oatmeal Served with Yogurt and Fresh Fruit

★★★☆☆

🕐 5 Minutes   ♨🕐 10 Minutes   🍴 1 servings

INGREDIENTS

- 1/2 cup rolled oats
- 1 cup water or milk
- Pinch of salt
- 1/2 cup Greek yogurt
- 1/2 cup mixed fresh fruit (such as berries, sliced banana, or diced apple)
- 1 tablespoon honey (optional)

INSTRUCTIONS

1. Bring the water or milk to a boil in a small saucepan. Add the oats and a pinch of salt, then reduce the heat to low.
2. Simmer uncovered for 10 minutes, stirring occasionally, until the oats are soft and have absorbed most of the liquid.
3. Transfer the cooked oats to a bowl and let cool slightly.
4. Top with Greek yogurt and fresh fruit.
5. Drizzle with honey if desired and serve immediately.

Nutritional : Calories: 350 kcal | Protein: 15 g | Carbohydrates: 55 g | Fat: 7 g | Fiber: 6 g | Sugar: 18 g

8. Oatmeal Topped with Sliced Bananas and Nuts

★★★☆☆

🕐 5 Minutes   ♨🕐 10 Minutes   🍴 1 servings

INGREDIENTS

- 1/2 cup rolled oats
- 1 cup almond milk
- Pinch of cinnamon
- 1 banana, sliced
- 1/4 cup mixed nuts, chopped (such as almonds, walnuts, and pecans)
- 1 tablespoon maple syrup (optional)

INSTRUCTIONS

1. In a small saucepan, bring the almond milk to a boil. Add the oats and cinnamon, and reduce heat to low.
2. Cook for about 10 minutes, stirring occasionally, until the oats are soft and creamy.
3. Pour the oatmeal into a serving bowl.
4. Top with sliced banana and chopped nuts.
5. Drizzle with maple syrup if desired and serve warm.

Nutritional : Calories: 340 kcal | Protein: 21 g | Carbohydrates: 3 g | Fat: 27 g | Fiber: 1 g | Sugar: 2 g

9. Smoked Salmon Avocado Toast

⭐⭐⭐☆☆

🕐 5 Minutes   🍳🕐 10 Minutes   🍴 1 servings

INGREDIENTS

- 1 slice of whole grain bread, toasted
- 1/2 avocado, mashed
- 2 ounces smoked salmon
- 1 tablespoon cream cheese
- Fresh dill for garnish
- Lemon wedge for serving
- Freshly cracked black pepper

INSTRUCTIONS

1. Spread the mashed avocado evenly on the toasted bread.
2. Layer the smoked salmon over the avocado.
3. Dollop cream cheese on top and sprinkle with fresh dill.
4. Serve with a wedge of lemon and freshly cracked black pepper.

Nutritional : Calories: 370 kcal | Protein: 23 g | Carbohydrates: 30 g | Fat: 18 g | Fiber: 7 g | Sugar: 3 g

10. Oat Bowl with Crunchy Almonds and Sweet Honey

⭐⭐⭐☆☆

🕐 5 Minutes   🍳🕐 10 Minutes   🍴 1 servings

INSTRUCTIONS

1. In a small saucepan, bring the water to a boil. Add the oats and salt, then reduce heat to low.
2. Cook, stirring occasionally, until the oats are creamy and have absorbed the water, about 10 minutes.
3. Transfer to a serving bowl.
4. Top with sliced almonds and sprinkle with cinnamon.
5. Drizzle honey over the top and serve warm.

INGREDIENTS

- 1/2 cup rolled oats
- 1 cup water
- Pinch of salt
- 1/4 cup sliced almonds
- 2 tablespoons honey
- 1/4 teaspoon cinnamon

Nutritional : Calories: 385 kcal | Protein: 10 g | Carbohydrates: 65 g | Fat: 12 g | Fiber: 6 g | Sugar: 24 g

11. Colorful Fresh Mixed Berry Fruit Salad

★★☆☆☆

5 Minutes   **0 Minutes**   **2 servings**

INSTRUCTIONS

1. In a large bowl, combine all the berries.
2. Drizzle with fresh orange juice and honey if using, then gently toss to coat the berries.
3. Sprinkle chopped fresh mint over the top for a refreshing flavor.
4. Serve immediately or chill in the refrigerator before serving for a refreshing summer breakfast.

INGREDIENTS

- 1 cup strawberries, hulled and halved
- 1/2 cup blueberries
- 1/2 cup raspberries
- 1/2 cup blackberries
- Juice of 1 orange
- 1 tablespoon chopped fresh mint
- 1 tablespoon honey (optional)

Nutritional : Calories: 110 kcal | Protein: 2 g | Carbohydrates: 27 g | Fat: 1 g | Fiber: 7 g | Sugar: 18 g

12. Creamy Vegan Asparagus Risotto with Lemon Zest

★★★☆☆

10 Minutes   **25 Minutes**   **2 servings**

INSTRUCTIONS

1. Heat the olive oil in a large pan over medium heat. Add the onion and cook until translucent.
2. Add the Arborio rice, stirring to coat with the oil and toast slightly, about 2 minutes.
3. Begin adding the warm vegetable broth one ladle at a time, stirring continuously until the liquid is absorbed before adding more.
4. When half the broth has been incorporated, add the asparagus.
5. Continue adding broth and stirring until the rice is creamy and al dente, and all the broth is absorbed.
6. Stir in the lemon zest, salt, and pepper.
7. Serve hot, garnished with fresh parsley.

INGREDIENTS

- 1 tablespoon olive oil
- 1 small onion, finely chopped
- 1 cup Arborio rice
- 1/2 pound asparagus, trimmed and cut into 1-inch pieces
- 3 cups vegetable broth, warmed
- Zest of 1 lemon
- Salt and pepper to taste
- Fresh parsley, chopped (for garnish)

Nutritional: Calories: 350 kcal | Protein: 9 g | Carbohydrates: 65 g | Fat: 7 g | Fiber: 4 g | Sugar: 4 g

13. Date-Goat Cheese Crostini

 10 Minutes  5 Minutes   4 servings

INGREDIENTS

- 1 baguette, sliced into 1/2-inch thick rounds
- 1 tablespoon olive oil
- 1/2 cup soft goat cheese
- 1/4 cup chopped dates
- Fresh thyme leaves for garnish

INSTRUCTIONS

1. Preheat the oven to 375°F (190°C).
2. Brush each baguette slice with olive oil and place on a baking sheet.
3. Bake in the preheated oven until lightly toasted, about 5 minutes.
4. Remove from oven and while still warm, spread each slice with goat cheese.
5. Top with chopped dates and sprinkle with fresh thyme leaves.
6. Serve immediately while warm.

Nutritional : Calories: 180 kcal | Protein: 6 g | Carbohydrates: 20 g | Fat: 8 g | Fiber: 1 g | Sugar: 10 g

14. Greek Yogurt and Spiced Apples

5 Minutes 10 Minutes 1 servings

INGREDIENTS

- 1 cup Greek yogurt
- 1 apple, cored and sliced
- 1 tablespoon honey
- 1/2 teaspoon ground cinnamon
- 1/4 teaspoon ground nutmeg
- A handful of walnuts, chopped
- Instructions:

INSTRUCTIONS

1. In a small skillet, combine the sliced apple, honey, cinnamon, and nutmeg. Cook over medium heat until the apples are soft and caramelized, about 10 minutes.
2. Place Greek yogurt in a serving bowl.
3. Top with the spiced apple mixture and sprinkle with chopped walnuts.
4. Serve immediately for a warm, comforting breakfast.

Nutritional: Calories: 290 kcal | Protein: 15 g | Carbohydrates: 42 g | Fat: 8 g | Fiber: 5 g | Sugar: 32 g

15. Oat Banana Pancake with Yogurt and Nuts

★★☆☆☆

10 Minutes   **10 Minutes**   **2 servings**

INSTRUCTIONS

1. In a blender, combine the mashed banana, rolled oats, eggs, baking powder, and milk. Blend until smooth.
2. Heat a non-stick skillet over medium heat. Pour about 1/4 cup of batter for each pancake and cook until bubbles form on the surface, then flip and cook until golden brown on both sides.
3. Serve the pancakes topped with Greek yogurt and chopped nuts.
4. Drizzle with maple syrup if desired.

INGREDIENTS

- 1 ripe banana, mashed
- 1 cup rolled oats
- 1/2 cup plain Greek yogurt
- 2 eggs
- 1/2 teaspoon baking powder
- 1/4 cup milk
- 1/4 cup mixed nuts, chopped
- Maple syrup for serving

Nutritional: Calories: 350 kcal | Protein: 18 g | Carbohydrates: 45 g | Fat: 12 g | Fiber: 6 g | Sugar: 12 g

16. Roasted Garlic Hummus Drizzled with Olive Oil

★★★★☆

10 Minutes   **40 Minutes**   **6 servings**

INSTRUCTIONS

1. Preheat the oven to 400°F (200°C). Cut the top off the head of garlic, drizzle with a little olive oil, wrap in foil, and roast for 40 minutes.
2. Once cooled, squeeze the roasted garlic cloves into a food processor.
3. Add chickpeas, 1/4 cup olive oil, tahini, and lemon juice to the food processor. Blend until smooth.
4. Season with salt and pepper.
5. Transfer to a serving dish, drizzle with additional olive oil, and sprinkle with paprika.
6. Serve with vegetables, pita bread, or as a spread.

INGREDIENTS

- 1 can (15 oz) chickpeas, drained and rinsed
- 1 head garlic
- 1/4 cup olive oil, plus more for drizzling
- 2 tablespoons tahini
- Juice of 1 lemon
- Salt and pepper to taste
- Paprika for garnish

Nutritional: Calories: 200 kcal | Protein: 6 g | Carbohydrates: 20 g | Fat: 12 g | Fiber: 5 g | Sugar: 3 g

GRAINS, LEGUME

17. Mediterranean Farro Salad with Olives and Tomatoes

 10 Minutes   10 Minutes   2 servings

INGREDIENTS

- 1 cup farro, rinsed
- 3 cups water
- 1 cup cherry tomatoes, halved
- 1/2 cup Kalamata olives, pitted and halved
- 1/4 cup red onion, finely chopped
- 1/4 cup fresh basil leaves, chopped
- 3 tablespoons olive oil
- 2 tablespoons balsamic vinegar
- Salt and pepper to taste
- Feta cheese, crumbled (optional)

INSTRUCTIONS

1. In a medium saucepan, combine farro and water. Bring to a boil, reduce heat to low, and simmer until farro is tender, about 30 minutes. Drain and let cool.
2. In a large bowl, combine cooked farro, cherry tomatoes, olives, red onion, and basil.
3. Whisk together olive oil and balsamic vinegar, then pour over the salad. Toss to combine.
4. Season with salt and pepper, and sprinkle with feta cheese if using.
5. Serve chilled or at room temperature.

Nutritional: Calories: 300 kcal | Protein: 8 g | Carbohydrates: 40 g | Fat: 12 g | Fiber: 8 g | Sugar: 5 g

18. Savory Vegan Mushroom Risotto with Arborio Rice and Thyme

 10 Minutes  25 Minutes   4 servings

INGREDIENTS

- 2 tablespoons olive oil
- 1 small onion, finely chopped
- 2 cloves garlic, minced
- 1 pound mushrooms, sliced
- 1 cup Arborio rice
- 4 cups vegetable broth, heated
- 1 teaspoon fresh thyme
- Salt and pepper to taste

INSTRUCTIONS

1. Heat olive oil in a large saucepan over medium heat. Add onion and garlic, sauté until soft.
2. Add mushrooms and cook until they release their moisture and begin to brown.
3. Stir in Arborio rice to mix with the mushrooms and onions.
4. Gradually add the heated vegetable broth one cup at a time, stirring continuously until the broth is absorbed before adding more.
5. Once the rice is creamy and just tender, stir in thyme, and season with salt and pepper.
6. Serve hot, garnished with additional herbs if desired.

Nutritional: Calories: 350 kcal | Protein: 9 g | Carbohydrates: 58 g | Fat: 10 g | Fiber: 3 g | Sugar: 4 g

19. Mediterranean Chickpea Salad with Feta and Olives

★★★☆☆

🕐 10 Minutes | ♨🕐 0 Minutes | 🍴 4 servings

INGREDIENTS

- 2 cans (15 oz each) chickpeas, rinsed and drained
- 1 cup cherry tomatoes, halved
- 1/2 cup Kalamata olives, pitted and sliced
- 1/2 red onion, thinly sliced
- 1/2 cup feta cheese, crumbled
- 1/4 cup fresh parsley, chopped
- 1/4 cup olive oil
- 2 tablespoons lemon juice
- 1 teaspoon dried oregano
- Salt and pepper to taste

INSTRUCTIONS

1. In a large bowl, combine chickpeas, cherry tomatoes, olives, red onion, and feta cheese.
2. In a small bowl, whisk together olive oil, lemon juice, oregano, salt, and pepper.
3. Pour the dressing over the salad and toss to combine.
4. Garnish with fresh parsley before serving.
5. Serve chilled or at room temperature for best flavor.

Nutritional: Calories: 345 kcal | Protein: 12 g | Carbohydrates: 30 g | Fat: 20 g | Fiber: 8 g | Sugar: 5 g

20. Chickpea Salad with Cucumbers, Tomatoes, and Red Onions

★★★☆☆

🕐 10 Minutes | ♨🕐 25 Minutes | 🍴 4 servings

INSTRUCTIONS

1. In a large bowl, combine chickpeas, cucumber, cherry tomatoes, and red onion.
2. In a small bowl, whisk together olive oil, red wine vinegar, dill, salt, and pepper.
3. Pour the dressing over the salad and toss to combine thoroughly.
4. Let the salad marinate for at least 30 minutes in the refrigerator before serving to enhance the flavors.
5. Serve chilled, garnished with additional dill if desired.

INGREDIENTS

- 2 cans (15 oz each) chickpeas, rinsed and drained
- 1 large cucumber, diced
- 1 cup cherry tomatoes, halved
- 1/2 red onion, thinly sliced
- 1/4 cup olive oil
- 2 tablespoons red wine vinegar
- 1 tablespoon fresh dill, chopped
- Salt and pepper to taste

Nutritional: Calories: 330 kcal | Protein: 10 g | Carbohydrates: 40 g | Fat: 15 g | Fiber: 10 g | Sugar: 8 g

21. Haricot Beans in Tomato Sauce

★★★☆☆

5 Minutes   20 Minutes   4 servings

INGREDIENTS

- 2 cans (15 oz each) haricot beans, rinsed and drained
- 1 tablespoon olive oil
- 1 small onion, finely chopped
- 2 cloves garlic, minced
- 1 can (14 oz) crushed tomatoes
- 1 teaspoon dried basil
- Salt and pepper to taste

INSTRUCTIONS

1. Heat olive oil in a saucepan over medium heat. Add onion and garlic and sauté until softened, about 5 minutes.
2. Add crushed tomatoes and dried basil, bringing to a simmer.
3. Stir in haricot beans and season with salt and pepper.
4. Simmer for 15 minutes to allow flavors to meld.
5. Serve hot, perfect as a side dish or a light main course.

Nutritional: Calories: 250 kcal | Protein: 8 g | Carbohydrates: 38 g | Fat: 7 g | Fiber: 10 g | Sugar: 6 g

22. Quinoa Tabbouleh with Cherry Tomatoes

★★★★☆

15 Minutes   15 Minutes   4 servings

INGREDIENTS

- 1 cup quinoa, rinsed
- 2 cups water
- 1 cup cherry tomatoes, halved
- 1 cucumber, diced
- 1/4 cup fresh parsley, finely chopped
- 1/4 cup fresh mint, finely chopped
- 1/4 cup lemon juice
- 1/4 cup olive oil
- Salt and pepper to taste

INSTRUCTIONS

1. In a saucepan, bring water to a boil. Add quinoa, reduce heat to low, cover, and cook for 15 minutes, or until water is absorbed. Let cool.
2. In a large bowl, combine cooked quinoa, cherry tomatoes, cucumber, parsley, and mint.
3. In a small bowl, whisk together lemon juice, olive oil, salt, and pepper.
4. Pour dressing over quinoa mixture and toss to combine.
5. Refrigerate for at least 30 minutes before serving to allow flavors to meld.
6. Serve chilled, garnished with additional herbs if desired.

Nutritional: Calories: 280 kcal | Protein: 6 g | Carbohydrates: 32 g | Fat: 14 g | Fiber: 5 g | Sugar: 4 g

23. Lentil Soup with Carrots, Celery, and Spinach

★★★☆☆

🕐 5 Minutes   🍳🕐 20 Minutes   🍴 4 servings

INGREDIENTS

- 1 cup dried lentils, rinsed
- 1 tablespoon olive oil
- 1 onion, chopped
- 2 carrots, diced
- 2 celery stalks, diced
- 3 cloves garlic, minced
- 6 cups vegetable broth
- 2 cups fresh spinach leaves
- Salt and pepper to taste
- 1 teaspoon dried thyme

INSTRUCTIONS

1. Heat olive oil in a large pot over medium heat. Add onion, carrots, celery, and garlic. Cook until vegetables are softened, about 10 minutes.
2. Add lentils, vegetable broth, and thyme. Bring to a boil, then reduce heat and simmer for 30 minutes, or until lentils are tender.
3. Stir in spinach and cook until wilted, about 5 minutes.
4. Season with salt and pepper.
5. Serve hot, with crusty bread if desired.

Nutritional: Calories: 240 kcal | Protein: 14 g | Carbohydrates: 35 g | Fat: 5 g | Fiber: 15 g | Sugar: 6 g

24. Asparagus Lemon Risotto with Parmesan

★★★☆☆

🕐 10 Minutes   🍳🕐 25 Minuten   🍴 4 servings

INGREDIENTS

- 1 tablespoon olive oil
- 1 small onion, finely chopped
- 2 cups Arborio rice
- 1/2 pound asparagus, trimmed and cut into 1-inch pieces
- 4 cups vegetable broth, heated
- Zest and juice of 1 lemon
- 1/2 cup grated Parmesan cheese
- Salt and pepper to taste

INSTRUCTIONS

1. Heat olive oil in a large pan over medium heat. Add the onion and cook until translucent.
2. Add Arborio rice, stirring to coat with the oil.
3. Begin adding the heated vegetable broth one cup at a time, stirring continuously until each cup is absorbed before adding the next.
4. Halfway through, add the asparagus pieces.
5. Once the rice is creamy and al dente, stir in lemon zest, lemon juice, and Parmesan cheese.
6. Season with salt and pepper to taste.
7. Serve hot, garnished with additional Parmesan if desired.

Nutritional: Calories: 430 kcal | Protein: 12 g | Carbohydrates: 68 g | Fat: 12 g | Fiber: 3 g | Sugar: 4 g

INGREDIENTS

- 1 cup quinoa, rinsed
- 2 cups water
- 1 can (15 oz) chickpeas, drained and rinsed
- 1 cucumber, diced
- 1 red bell pepper, diced
- 1/4 cup red onion, finely chopped
- 1/4 cup tahini
- 2 tablespoons lemon juice
- 1 garlic clove, minced
- 2 tablespoons warm water
- Salt and pepper to taste
- Fresh parsley, chopped (for garnish)

25. Quinoa and Chickpea Salad with Lemon Tahini Dressing

15 Minutes   15 Minutes   4 servings

INSTRUCTIONS

1. In a saucepan, bring 2 cups of water to a boil. Add quinoa, reduce heat to low, cover, and simmer for 15 minutes, or until all water is absorbed. Remove from heat and let sit covered for 5 minutes. Fluff with a fork and let cool.
2. In a large bowl, combine cooked quinoa, chickpeas, cucumber, red bell pepper, and red onion.
3. In a small bowl, whisk together tahini, lemon juice, minced garlic, and warm water until smooth. Add salt and pepper to taste.
4. Pour the dressing over the salad and toss to coat evenly.
5. Refrigerate for at least 30 minutes to allow flavors to blend.
6. Serve chilled, garnished with chopped parsley.

Nutritional: Calories: 340 kcal | Protein: 13 g | Carbohydrates: 49 g | Fat: 12 g | Fiber: 9 g | Sugar: 5 g

INGREDIENTS

- 4 large zucchinis, spiralized
- 1 tablespoon olive oil
- 2 cups marinara sauce
- 1/4 cup vegan parmesan cheese, grated
- Salt and pepper to taste
- Fresh basil, for garnish

26. Zucchini Noodles with Flavorful Marinara Sauce and Vegan Parmesan

10 Minutes   20 Minutes   4 servings

INSTRUCTIONS

1. Heat olive oil in a large skillet over medium heat. Add spiralized zucchini noodles and sauté for 3-5 minutes, just until tender.
2. Add marinara sauce to the skillet, stirring to coat the noodles. Cook for an additional 5 minutes, allowing the flavors to meld.
3. Season with salt and pepper.
4. Serve hot, sprinkled with vegan parmesan and garnished with fresh basil.

Nutritional: Calories: 160 kcal | Protein: 4 g | Carbohydrates: 18 g | Fat: 8 g | Fiber: 4 g | Sugar: 10 g

27. Pasta with Basil Pesto and Cherry Tomatoes

⭐⭐⭐☆☆

🕐 10 Minutes   🍳🕐 10 Minutes   🍴 4 servings

INSTRUCTIONS

1. Cook pasta according to package instructions until al dente. Drain and return to the pot.
2. Stir in basil pesto and cherry tomatoes, mixing until the pasta is evenly coated.
3. Season with salt and pepper.
4. Serve warm, garnished with grated Parmesan cheese.

INGREDIENTS

- 12 oz pasta (e.g., spaghetti or fettuccine)
- 1 cup basil pesto (homemade or store-bought)
- 1 cup cherry tomatoes, halved
- Salt and pepper to taste
- Grated Parmesan cheese, for garnish

Nutritional: Calories: 410 kcal | Protein: 12 g | Carbohydrates: 56 g | Fat: 16 g | Fiber: 4 g | Sugar: 3 g

28. Pasta with Garlic Shrimp Scampi

⭐⭐⭐⭐☆

🕐 10 Minutes   🍳🕐 10 Minutes   🍴 4 servings

INSTRUCTIONS

1. Cook pasta according to package instructions until al dente. Drain and set aside.
2. In a large skillet, heat olive oil over medium heat. Add garlic and sauté for 1 minute.
3. Add shrimp and cook until pink and opaque, about 2-3 minutes per side.
4. If using, pour in white wine and let simmer for 1 minute. Stir in lemon juice.
5. Toss the cooked pasta with the shrimp mixture.
6. Season with salt and pepper.
7. Serve garnished with chopped parsley.

INGREDIENTS

- 12 oz spaghetti or linguine
- 1 pound shrimp, peeled and deveined
- 3 tablespoons olive oil
- 3 cloves garlic, minced
- 1/2 cup white wine (optional)
- Juice of 1 lemon
- Salt and pepper to taste
- Fresh parsley, chopped (for garnish)

Nutritional: Calories: 460 kcal | Protein: 28 g | Carbohydrates: 56 g | Fat: 14 g | Fiber: 3 g | Sugar: 2 g

29. Grilled Zucchini and Eggplant

10 Minutes   10 Minutes   4 servings

INGREDIENTS

- 2 zucchinis, sliced lengthwise
- 2 eggplants, sliced lengthwise
- 2 tablespoons olive oil
- Salt and pepper to taste
- Fresh herbs (such as thyme or basil), for garnish

INSTRUCTIONS

1. Preheat the grill to medium-high heat.
2. Brush zucchini and eggplant slices with olive oil and season with salt and pepper.
3. Grill vegetables for about 5 minutes per side, until tender and grill marks appear.
4. Serve hot, garnished with fresh herbs.

Nutritional: Calories: 140 kcal | Protein: 3 g | Carbohydrates: 20 g | Fat: 7 g | Fiber: 9 g | Sugar: 11 g

30. Roasted Peppers with Garlic, Basil, and Tomato

10 Minutes   10 Minutes   4 servings

INGREDIENTS

- 4 bell peppers, assorted colors, halved and seeded
- 4 cloves garlic, minced
- 1 cup cherry tomatoes, halved
- 1/4 cup fresh basil, chopped
- 2 tablespoons olive oil
- Salt and pepper to taste

INSTRUCTIONS

1. Preheat the oven to 400°F (200°C).
2. Place the bell peppers cut-side up on a baking sheet.
3. In a bowl, mix together garlic, tomatoes, basil, and olive oil. Spoon the mixture into the bell pepper halves.
4. Season with salt and pepper.
5. Roast in the oven for 25 minutes, or until the peppers are tender.
6. Serve warm.

Nutritional: Calories: 150 kcal | Protein: 2 g | Carbohydrates: 18 g | Fat: 9 g | Fiber: 5 g | Sugar: 12 g

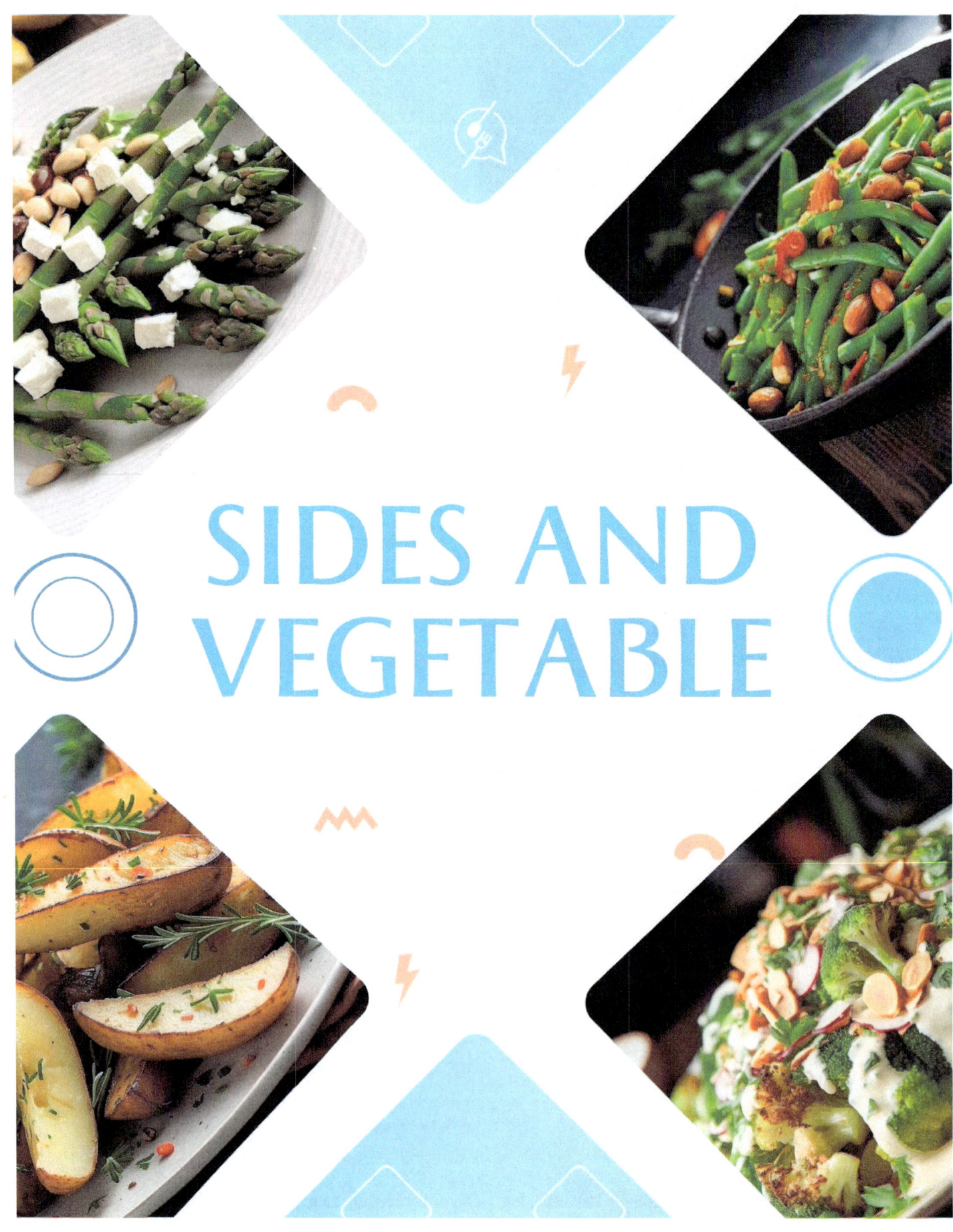

SIDES AND VEGETABLE

31. Vegan Eggplant Parmesan with Marinara Sauce and Cheese

★★★★★

15 Minutes   **30 Minutes**   **4 servings**

INGREDIENTS

- 2 large eggplants, sliced into 1/2-inch thick rounds
- 2 cups marinara sauce
- 2 cups vegan mozzarella cheese, shredded
- 1/2 cup vegan parmesan cheese, grated
- 1/4 cup fresh basil leaves, for garnish
- Salt and pepper to taste
- Olive oil for brushing

INSTRUCTIONS

1. Preheat the oven to 375°F (190°C).
2. Brush both sides of eggplant slices with olive oil and season with salt and pepper. Arrange on a baking sheet.
3. Bake for 15 minutes, flipping halfway through until slightly tender.
4. In a baking dish, layer a spoonful of marinara sauce, followed by a layer of eggplant slices, a sprinkle of vegan mozzarella, and a sprinkle of vegan parmesan. Repeat the layers until all ingredients are used.
5. Bake in the preheated oven for 15 minutes, or until the cheese is melted and bubbly.
6. Garnish with fresh basil leaves before serving.

Nutritional: Calories: 290 kcal | Protein: 16 g | Carbohydrates: 38 g | Fat: 10 g | Fiber: 12 g | Sugar: 18 g

32. Baked Potatoes with Rosemary and Sea Salt

★★★★☆

5 Minutes   **45 Minutes**   **4 servings**

INGREDIENTS

- 4 large potatoes, scrubbed
- 2 tablespoons olive oil
- 2 teaspoons fresh rosemary, finely chopped
- Sea salt, to taste

INSTRUCTIONS

1. Preheat the oven to 425°F (220°C).
2. Pierce the potatoes several times with a fork to allow steam to escape during baking.
3. Rub each potato with olive oil, then sprinkle with chopped rosemary and sea salt.
4. Place the potatoes directly on the middle oven rack and bake for 45 minutes, or until the potatoes are tender and the skin is crispy.
5. Serve hot, optionally with a side of Greek yogurt or sour cream.

Nutritional: Calories: 280 kcal | Protein: 6 g | Carbohydrates: 50 g | Fat: 7 g | Fiber: 4 g | Sugar: 2 g

33. Cucumber Salad with Tomatoes and Feta Cheese

★★☆☆☆

🕐 10 Minutes   🍳🕐 0 Minutes   🍴 4 servings

INSTRUCTIONS

1. In a large bowl, combine cucumbers, cherry tomatoes, feta cheese, and red onion.
2. Drizzle with olive oil and red wine vinegar, then toss to combine.
3. Season with salt and pepper.
4. Garnish with chopped dill before serving.
5. Serve chilled for a refreshing side dish.

INGREDIENTS

- 2 large cucumbers, diced
- 1 cup cherry tomatoes, halved
- 1/2 cup feta cheese, crumbled
- 1/4 cup red onion, thinly sliced
- 2 tablespoons olive oil
- 1 tablespoon red wine vinegar
- Salt and pepper to taste
- Fresh dill, chopped, for garnish

Nutritional: Calories: 160 kcal | Protein: 4 g | Carbohydrates: 10 g | Fat: 12 g | Fiber: 2 g | Sugar: 5 g

34. Salad with Asparagus, Feta Cheese, Pine Nuts, and Lemon

★★★★☆

🕐 15 Minutes   🍳🕐 10 Minutes   🍴 4 servings

INSTRUCTIONS

INGREDIENTS

- 1 pound asparagus, trimmed and cut into 1-inch pieces
- 1/2 cup pine nuts, toasted
- 1/2 cup feta cheese, crumbled
- Zest and juice of 1 lemon
- 1/4 cup olive oil
- Salt and pepper to taste

1. Bring a pot of salted water to a boil. Add asparagus and cook for 3 minutes until bright green and slightly tender. Drain and plunge into ice water to stop cooking.
2. In a large bowl, combine blanched asparagus, toasted pine nuts, and crumbled feta cheese.
3. In a small bowl, whisk together lemon zest, lemon juice, and olive oil. Season with salt and pepper.
4. Pour the dressing over the salad and toss gently.

Nutritional: Calories: 300 kcal | Protein: 8 g | Carbohydrates: 10 g | Fat: 27 g | Fiber: 3 g | Sugar: 4 g

35. Broccoli and Cauliflower Salad with Tahini Dressing

★★★☆☆

🕐 15 Minutes | 0 Minutes | 🍴 4 servings

INGREDIENTS

- 2 cups broccoli florets
- 2 cups cauliflower florets
- 1/4 cup tahini
- 2 tablespoons lemon juice
- 1 garlic clove, minced
- Water, as needed to thin the dressing
- Salt and pepper to taste
- 1/4 cup toasted slivered almonds

INSTRUCTIONS

1. In a large bowl, combine broccoli and cauliflower florets.
2. In a small bowl, whisk together tahini, lemon juice, minced garlic, and enough water to achieve a pourable consistency. Season with salt and pepper.
3. Drizzle the tahini dressing over the broccoli and cauliflower, tossing to coat evenly.
4. Sprinkle toasted slivered almonds on top before serving.
5. Serve chilled or at room temperature.

Nutritional: Calories: 220 kcal | Protein: 7 g | Carbohydrates: 15 g | Fat: 16 g | Fiber: 5 g | Sugar: 3 g

36. Chickpea Salad with Cucumbers, Tomatoes, and Red Onions

★★★★☆

🕐 10 Minutes | 0 Minutes | 🍴 4 servings

INGREDIENTS

- 2 cans (15 oz each) chickpeas, rinsed and drained
- 1 large cucumber, diced
- 1 cup cherry tomatoes, halved
- 1/2 red onion, thinly sliced
- 1/4 cup fresh parsley, chopped
- 3 tablespoons olive oil
- 2 tablespoons lemon juice
- Salt and pepper to taste

INSTRUCTIONS

1. In a large bowl, combine chickpeas, cucumber, cherry tomatoes, and red onion.
2. Add fresh parsley.
3. Drizzle with olive oil and lemon juice, then season with salt and pepper.
4. Toss all ingredients together until well combined.
5. Serve immediately or chill in the refrigerator to let flavors meld before serving.

Nutritional: Calories: 295 kcal | Protein: 10 g | Carbohydrates: 45 g | Fat: 9 g | Fiber: 12 g | Sugar: 8 g

37. Spicy Szechuan Stir-Fried Green Beans with Garlic and Chili Peppers

🕐 10 Minutes   〰🕐 10 Minutes   🍴 4 servings

INGREDIENTS

- 1 pound green beans, trimmed
- 2 tablespoons vegetable oil
- 3 cloves garlic, minced
- 2 red chili peppers, sliced
- 1 tablespoon soy sauce
- 1 teaspoon Szechuan peppercorns, crushed
- Salt to taste

INSTRUCTIONS

1. Heat oil in a large skillet or wok over high heat.
2. Add green beans and stir-fry for about 5 minutes, or until they start to blister.
3. Add garlic and chili peppers, continuing to stir-fry for another 2 minutes.
4. Stir in soy sauce and Szechuan peppercorns, cooking for an additional 1 minute.
5. Season with salt to taste.
6. Serve hot as a side dish or part of a larger meal.

Nutritional: Calories: 120 kcal | Protein: 3 g | Carbohydrates: 10 g | Fat: 8 g | Fiber: 3 g | Sugar: 4 g

38. Grilled Vegetable Salad with Zucchini, Eggplant, Onions, Peppers, and Tomato

🕐 15 Minutes   〰🕐 10 Minutes   🍴 4 servings

INGREDIENTS

- 1 zucchini, sliced
- 1 eggplant, sliced
- 1 red onion, sliced
- 1 red bell pepper, sliced
- 1 yellow bell pepper, sliced
- 2 tomatoes, sliced
- 1/4 cup olive oil
- Salt and pepper to taste
- 2 tablespoons balsamic vinegar
- Fresh basil leaves, for garnish

INSTRUCTIONS

1. Preheat grill to medium-high heat.
2. Brush vegetables with olive oil and season with salt and pepper.
3. Grill vegetables for about 5 minutes per side, or until tender and charred.
4. Arrange grilled vegetables on a platter.
5. Drizzle with balsamic vinegar.
6. Garnish with fresh basil leaves.
7. Serve warm or at room temperature.

Nutritional: Calories: 200 kcal | Protein: 3 g | Carbohydrates: 18 g | Fat: 14 g | Fiber: 5 g | Sugar: 10 g

39. Sautéed Spinach and Mushroom Salad

★★★★★

10 Minutes   10 Minutes   4 servings

INGREDIENTS

- 1 pound fresh spinach, washed and dried
- 1 cup mushrooms, sliced
- 2 tablespoons olive oil
- 2 cloves garlic, minced
- Salt and pepper to taste
- 2 tablespoons lemon juice
- 1/4 cup grated Parmesan cheese

INSTRUCTIONS

1. Heat olive oil in a large skillet over medium heat.
2. Add garlic and mushrooms, sautéing until mushrooms are browned and tender.
3. Add spinach and cook until just wilted.
4. Season with salt, pepper, and lemon juice.
5. Sprinkle with Parmesan cheese.
6. Serve immediately as a warm salad.

Nutritional: Calories: 130 kcal | Protein: 6 g | Carbohydrates: 6 g | Fat: 10 g | Fiber: 2 g | Sugar: 1 g

SEAFOOD

40. Grilled Salmon Fillet with Lemon and Dill Garnish

★★☆☆☆

🕐 **5 Minutes**　　♨🕐 **10 Minutes**　　🍴 **4 servings**

INSTRUCTIONS

1. Preheat grill to medium-high heat.
2. Brush salmon fillets with olive oil and season with salt and pepper.
3. Grill salmon, skin side down, for 5 minutes. Flip carefully and place lemon slices on top. Grill for another 5 minutes or until cooked through.
4. Remove from grill and garnish with fresh dill.
5. Serve immediately.

INGREDIENTS

- 4 salmon fillets (6 ounces each)
- 2 tablespoons olive oil
- Salt and pepper to taste
- 1 lemon, sliced
- Fresh dill, for garnish

Nutritional: Calories: 280 kcal | Protein: 23 g | Carbohydrates: 0 g | Fat: 20 g | Fiber: 0 g | Sugar: 0 g

41. Grilled Salmon Fillet with Fresh Salad

★★★☆☆

🕐 10 Minutes   🍳🕐 10 Minutes   🍴 4 servings

INGREDIENTS

- 4 salmon fillets (6 ounces each)
- 2 tablespoons olive oil
- Salt and pepper to taste
- 4 cups mixed greens
- 1/2 cup cherry tomatoes, halved
- 1/4 cup cucumber, sliced
- 2 tablespoons balsamic vinaigrette

INSTRUCTIONS

1. Preheat grill to medium-high heat.
2. Brush salmon fillets with olive oil and season with salt and pepper.
3. Grill salmon for 5 minutes on each side or until cooked through.
4. Toss mixed greens, cherry tomatoes, and cucumber with balsamic vinaigrette.
5. Serve grilled salmon on top of the fresh salad.

Nutritional: Calories: 310 kcal | Protein: 24 g | Carbohydrates: 4 g | Fat: 22 g | Fiber: 1 g | Sugar: 2 g

42. Shrimp Scampi Linguine with Cherry Tomatoes and Parsley

★★★★☆

🕐 5 Minutes   🍳🕐 10 Minutes   🍴 4 servings

INGREDIENTS

- 12 oz linguine
- 2 tablespoons olive oil
- 1 pound shrimp, peeled and deveined
- 4 cloves garlic, minced
- 1/2 cup white wine
- 1 cup cherry tomatoes, halved
- Salt and pepper to taste
- 1/4 cup fresh parsley, chopped

INSTRUCTIONS

1. Cook linguine according to package instructions until al dente. Drain and set aside.
2. In a large skillet, heat olive oil over medium heat. Add garlic and sauté for 1 minute.
3. Add shrimp and cook until pink and opaque, about 2-3 minutes per side.
4. Pour in white wine and add cherry tomatoes. Simmer for 2 minutes.
5. Toss cooked linguine with shrimp mixture. Season with salt and pepper.
6. Garnish with chopped parsley and serve immediately.

INGREDIENTS

- 1 medium octopus, cleaned (about 2 pounds)
- 1 lemon, halved
- 2 bay leaves
- 1 cup cherry tomatoes, halved
- 1/4 cup chopped fresh parsley
- 1/4 cup olive oil
- 2 tablespoons red wine vinegar
- Salt and pepper to taste

43. Octopus Salad with Tomatoes and Parsley

20 Minutes   120 Minutes   4 servings

INSTRUCTIONS

1. Place the octopus in a large pot with lemon halves and bay leaves. Cover with water and bring to a boil. Reduce heat and simmer gently for about 1.5 hours or until the octopus is tender.
2. Remove the octopus from the water and let it cool. Once cooled, cut into bite-sized pieces.
3. In a large bowl, combine the octopus, cherry tomatoes, and parsley.
4. Whisk together olive oil, red wine vinegar, salt, and pepper in a small bowl. Pour over the octopus salad and toss to combine.
5. Refrigerate for at least one hour to allow flavors to meld.
6. Serve chilled, garnished with additional parsley if desired.

Nutritional: Calories: 270 kcal | Protein: 25 g | Carbohydrates: 6 g | Fat: 16 g | Fiber: 2 g | Sugar: 2 g

INGREDIENTS

- 1 pound fresh tuna steak, sushi grade
- 2 cups mixed greens
- 1/2 cup sliced cucumber
- 1/2 cup cherry tomatoes, halved
- 1/4 cup finely diced red onion
- 2 tablespoons olive oil
- 1 tablespoon lemon juice
- Salt and pepper to taste

44. Fresh Raw Tuna with Vegetable Salad

15 Minutes   0 Minutes   4 servings

INSTRUCTIONS

1. Thinly slice the tuna steak against the grain.
2. Arrange mixed greens on plates. Top with sliced cucumber, cherry tomatoes, and red onion.
3. Place sliced tuna on top of the salad.
4. In a small bowl, whisk together olive oil, lemon juice, salt, and pepper.
5. Drizzle the dressing over the salad and tuna.
6. Serve immediately, ensuring the freshness of the tuna is preserved.

Nutritional: Calories: 220 kcal | Protein: 27 g | Carbohydrates: 5 g | Fat: 10 g | Fiber: 1 g | Sugar: 2 g

45. Grilled Shrimp and Pineapple Skewers with Sweet Chili Glaze

★★★☆☆

🕐 15 Minutes   ♨🕐 10 Minutes   🍴 4 servings

INSTRUCTIONS

1. Preheat grill to medium-high heat.
2. In a small bowl, mix sweet chili sauce, soy sauce, garlic, ginger, and lime juice.
3. Thread shrimp and pineapple chunks alternately onto skewers.
4. Brush the skewers with the chili sauce mixture.
5. Grill for 2-3 minutes per side or until shrimp are pink and cooked through.
6. Garnish with fresh cilantro before serving.

INGREDIENTS

- 1 pound large shrimp, peeled and deveined
- 1 cup pineapple, cut into chunks
- 1/4 cup sweet chili sauce
- 1 tablespoon soy sauce
- 1 teaspoon garlic, minced
- 1 teaspoon ginger, minced
- 2 tablespoons lime juice
- Fresh cilantro, for garnish

Nutritional: Calories: 210 kcal | Protein: 24 g | Carbohydrates: 18 g | Fat: 4 g | Fiber: 1 g | Sugar: 15 g

46. Crispy Fried Calamari Served with Lemon Wedges

★★★★☆

🕐 10 Minutes   ♨🕐 5 Minutes   🍴 4 servings

INSTRUCTIONS

1. In a large bowl, combine flour, paprika, salt, and pepper.
2. Toss calamari rings in the flour mixture until well coated.
3. Heat oil in a deep fryer or large pot to 375°F (190°C).
4. Fry calamari in batches until golden and crisp, about 2-3 minutes.
5. Drain on paper towels.
6. Serve hot with lemon wedges on the side for squeezing.

INGREDIENTS

- 1 pound calamari, cleaned and sliced into rings
- 1 cup all-purpose flour
- 1 teaspoon paprika
- Salt and pepper to taste
- Vegetable oil, for frying
- Lemon wedges, for serving

Nutritional: Calories: 310 kcal | Protein: 18 g | Carbohydrates: 28 g | Fat: 14 g | Fiber: 1 g | Sugar: 1 g

47. Stir-Fried Mixed Vegetables with Shrimp

★★★☆☆

10 Minutes   10 Minutes   4 servings

INGREDIENTS

- 1 pound shrimp, peeled and deveined
- 2 tablespoons vegetable oil
- 1 red bell pepper, sliced
- 1 green bell pepper, sliced
- 1 onion, sliced
- 2 cloves garlic, minced
- 2 tablespoons soy sauce
- 1 tablespoon oyster sauce
- 1 teaspoon sesame oil
- Salt and pepper to taste

INSTRUCTIONS

1. Heat vegetable oil in a large skillet or wok over medium-high heat.
2. Add garlic and onion, sauté for 2 minutes until fragrant.
3. Add red and green bell peppers, cook for an additional 3 minutes.
4. Add shrimp and stir-fry until they turn pink and are cooked through, about 3-4 minutes.
5. Stir in soy sauce, oyster sauce, and sesame oil. Mix well.
6. Season with salt and pepper.
7. Serve hot, ideally over a bed of steamed rice.

Nutritional: Calories: 240 kcal | Protein: 24 g | Carbohydrates: 9 g | Fat: 12 g | Fiber: 2 g | Sugar: 4 g

48. Pike Perch Fillet with Grilled Zucchini and White Sauce

★★★★★

15 Minutes   20 Minutes   4 servings

INGREDIENTS

- For the Fish:
- 4 pike perch fillets
- 2 tablespoons olive oil
- Salt and pepper to taste
- 1 teaspoon paprika
- 1 teaspoon dried thyme
- For the Zucchini:
- 2 medium zucchinis, sliced
- 2 tablespoons olive oil
- Salt and pepper to taste
- 1 teaspoon dried oregano

INSTRUCTIONS

1. Preheat the Oven: Preheat your oven to 200 degrees Celsius (390 degrees Fahrenheit) for the fish. Preheat a grill or grill pan for the zucchini.
2. Prepare the Fish: Rub the pike perch fillets with olive oil, and season with salt, pepper, paprika, and thyme. Place the fillets on a baking sheet lined with parchment paper. Bake in the preheated oven for 15-20 minutes, or until the fish is opaque and flakes easily with a fork.
3. Grill the Zucchini: Toss the zucchini slices with olive oil, salt, pepper, and oregano. Grill the zucchini slices for about 3-4 minutes on each side until tender and grill marks appear. Set aside and keep warm.

Nutritional: Calories: 280 kcal | Protein: 32 g | Carbohydrates: 6 g | Fat: 14 g | Fiber: 2 g | Sugar: 3 g

49. Grilled Fish with Roasted Potatoes and Vegetables

★★★☆☆

🕐 15 Minutes   🍳🕐 30 Minutes   🍴 4 servings

INSTRUCTIONS

1. Preheat your grill to medium-high heat and preheat the oven to 400°F (200°C) for the vegetables.
2. Toss the potatoes and vegetables with 2 tablespoons of olive oil, garlic powder, salt, and pepper. Spread on a baking sheet and roast in the oven for 20-25 minutes, stirring halfway through, until tender and lightly browned.
3. Brush the fish fillets with the remaining olive oil and season with salt and pepper. Grill the fish for about 4-5 minutes per side, depending on thickness, until cooked through and flaky.
4. Serve the grilled fish alongside the roasted potatoes and vegetables. Garnish with fresh parsley.

INGREDIENTS

- 4 white fish fillets (such as cod or halibut, about 6 ounces each)
- 4 tablespoons olive oil
- 2 teaspoons garlic powder
- Salt and pepper to taste
- 1 pound baby potatoes, halved
- 1 red bell pepper, sliced
- 1 yellow bell pepper, sliced
- 1 zucchini, sliced
- Fresh parsley, chopped for garnish

Nutritional: Calories: 390 kcal | Protein: 28 g | Carbohydrates: 28 g | Fat: 19 g | Fiber: 5 g | Sugar: 4 g

50. Risotto with Shrimp

★★★★☆

🕐 10 Minutes   🍳🕐 25 Minutes   🍴 4 servings

INSTRUCTIONS

1. Heat olive oil in a large skillet over medium heat. Add the onion and sauté until translucent, about 3-4 minutes.
2. Add the Arborio rice and stir for 2 minutes to lightly toast the grains.
3. Pour in the white wine and stir until absorbed.
4. Begin adding the warm broth, one ladle at a time, stirring constantly until each addition is absorbed before adding the next.
5. When the rice is almost done (about 18 minutes), add the shrimp and cook until they are pink and cooked through, about 5-7 minutes.
6. Stir in the Parmesan cheese and season with salt and pepper to taste.
7. Serve hot, garnished with chopped parsley.

INGREDIENTS

- 1 tablespoon olive oil
- 1 small onion, finely chopped
- 2 cups Arborio rice
- 1/2 cup white wine
- 4 cups seafood or vegetable broth, kept warm
- 1 pound shrimp, peeled and deveined
- 1/2 cup grated Parmesan cheese
- Salt and pepper to taste
- Fresh parsley, chopped for garnish

Nutritional: Calories: 520 kcal | Protein: 32 g | Carbohydrates: 64 g | Fat: 14 g | Fiber: 2 g | Sugar: 2 g

51. Seafood Pasta Paella

★★★☆☆

🕐 15 Minutes   🍳🕐 30 Minutes   🍴 4 servings

INGREDIENTS

- 1 tablespoon olive oil
- 1 onion, chopped
- 2 cloves garlic, minced
- 1 teaspoon paprika
- 1/2 teaspoon saffron threads
- 1 cup Arborio rice or short-grain rice
- 3 cups seafood broth
- 1 cup mixed seafood (shrimp, mussels, and clams)
- 1/2 cup peas
- Salt and pepper to taste
- Lemon wedges for serving

INSTRUCTIONS

1. Heat olive oil in a large skillet or paella pan over medium heat. Add onion and garlic, and cook until softened.
2. Stir in paprika and saffron, then add the rice, coating well with the oil and spices.
3. Pour in the seafood broth and bring to a boil. Reduce heat to low and simmer, covered, for about 20 minutes.
4. Add the mixed seafood and peas, and cook until the seafood is cooked through and rice is tender, about 10 minutes.
5. Season with salt and pepper.
6. Serve hot with lemon wedges on the side for squeezing.

Nutritional: Calories: 360 kcal | Protein: 24 g | Carbohydrates: 48 g | Fat: 8 g | Fiber: 3 g | Sugar: 3 g

52. Baked Halibut with Red Sauce

★★★★☆

🕐 10 Minutes   🍳🕐 25 Minutes   🍴 4 servings

INGREDIENTS

- 4 halibut fillets (6 ounces each)
- 2 tablespoons olive oil
- 1 onion, finely chopped
- 2 garlic cloves, minced
- 1 can (14 oz) crushed tomatoes
- 1 teaspoon dried basil
- 1 teaspoon dried oregano
- Salt and pepper to taste
- Fresh basil for garnish

INSTRUCTIONS

1. Preheat oven to 375°F (190°C).
2. Heat olive oil in a skillet over medium heat. Add onion and garlic, and sauté until soft and translucent.
3. Add crushed tomatoes, dried basil, and oregano. Simmer for 5 minutes. Season with salt and pepper.
4. Place the halibut fillets in a baking dish. Pour the tomato sauce over the fillets.
5. Bake in the preheated oven for 15-20 minutes, or until the fish flakes easily with a fork.
6. Garnish with fresh basil leaves before serving.

Nutritional: Calories: 280 kcal | Protein: 23 g | Carbohydrates: 8 g | Fat: 17 g | Fiber: 2 g | Sugar: 4 g

INGREDIENTS

- 8 oz linguine
- 2 tablespoons olive oil
- 1/2 pound shrimp, peeled and deveined
- 1/2 pound scallops
- 2 cloves garlic, minced
- 1/2 cup white wine
- 1 lemon, juiced
- Salt and pepper to taste
- Fresh parsley, chopped for garnish

53. Linguine with Shrimp and Scallops

★★★☆☆

🕐 10 Minutes   🍳🕐 30 Minutes   🍴 4 servings

INSTRUCTIONS

1. Cook linguine according to package directions until al dente. Drain and set aside.
2. Heat olive oil in a large skillet over medium-high heat. Add garlic and sauté for 1 minute.
3. Add shrimp and scallops to the skillet. Cook for 2-3 minutes per side until they are just cooked through and golden.
4. Pour in white wine and lemon juice, simmer for 2 minutes to let the alcohol evaporate.
5. Toss the cooked linguine with the shrimp, scallops, and sauce. Season with salt and pepper.
6. Serve garnished with chopped parsley.

Nutritional: Calories: 360 kcal | Protein: 24 g | Carbohydrates: 48 g | Fat: 8 g | Fiber: 3 g | Sugar: 3 g

INGREDIENTS

- 4 striped bass fillets (6 ounces each)
- 2 tablespoons olive oil
- 1 lemon, sliced
- 2 tablespoons fresh herbs (such as parsley, thyme, or dill), chopped
- Salt and pepper to taste

54. Grilled Striped Bass with Lemon and Herb

★★★★☆

🕐 10 Minutes   🍳🕐 25 Minutes   🍴 4 servings

INSTRUCTIONS

1. Preheat grill to medium-high heat.
2. Brush both sides of the bass fillets with olive oil. Season with salt and pepper.
3. Place lemon slices and a sprinkle of fresh herbs on each fillet.
4. Grill the fish, skin side down, without flipping, for about 10 minutes, or until the fish is opaque and flakes easily with a fork.
5. Serve hot, garnished with additional fresh herbs.

Nutritional: Calories: 230 kcal | Protein: 23 g | Carbohydrates: 2 g | Fat: 14 g | Fiber: 0.5 g | Sugar: 0.5 g

55. Baked Fillet of Sea Bream with Vegetables

★★★★☆

15 Minutes   25 Minutes   4 servings

INGREDIENTS

- 4 sea bream fillets (6 ounces each)
- 2 tablespoons olive oil
- 1 zucchini, sliced
- 1 red bell pepper, sliced
- 1 yellow bell pepper, sliced
- 1 small red onion, sliced
- 2 cloves garlic, minced
- 1 lemon, sliced
- Salt and pepper to taste
- Fresh herbs (such as thyme or rosemary), for garnish

INSTRUCTIONS

1. Preheat the oven to 375°F (190°C).
2. Arrange the sliced vegetables and garlic in a baking dish, and drizzle with 1 tablespoon of olive oil. Season with salt and pepper.
3. Place the sea bream fillets on top of the vegetables. Season with salt and pepper, and place lemon slices on top of each fillet.
4. Drizzle the remaining olive oil over the fish.
5. Bake in the preheated oven for 20-25 minutes, or until the fish is cooked through and vegetables are tender.
6. Garnish with fresh herbs before serving.

Nutritional: Calories: 290 kcal | Protein: 25 g | Carbohydrates: 12 g | Fat: 16 g | Fiber: 3 g | Sugar: 5 g

56. Mixed Salad with Shrimps, Avocado, and Cherry Tomatoes

★★☆☆☆

10 Minutes   0 Minutes   4 servings

INGREDIENTS

- 1 pound cooked shrimp, peeled and deveined
- 2 avocados, diced
- 1 cup cherry tomatoes, halved
- 1/4 cup red onion, thinly sliced
- 1/4 cup cilantro, chopped
- 2 tablespoons olive oil
- Juice of 1 lime
- Salt and pepper to taste

INSTRUCTIONS

1. In a large bowl, combine shrimp, avocados, cherry tomatoes, red onion, and cilantro.
2. In a small bowl, whisk together olive oil, lime juice, salt, and pepper.
3. Pour the dressing over the salad and toss gently to combine.
4. Serve immediately, ensuring the salad is fresh and vibrant.

Nutritional: Calories: 350 kcal | Protein: 25 g | Carbohydrates: 14 g | Fat: 22 g | Fiber: 7 g | Sugar: 3 g

INGREDIENTS

- 4 salmon fillets (6 ounces each)
- 2 tablespoons olive oil
- 2 avocados, diced
- 1 cup cherry tomatoes, halved
- 1/4 cup red onion, thinly sliced
- 1/4 cup fresh basil, chopped
- 2 tablespoons balsamic vinegar
- Salt and pepper to taste

57. Salmon Avocado and Tomato Salad

★★☆☆☆

🕐 10 Minutes   🍳🕐 10 Minutes   🍴 4 servings

INSTRUCTIONS

1. Preheat grill to medium-high heat.
2. Brush salmon with 1 tablespoon olive oil, season with salt and pepper, and grill for about 5 minutes per side, or until fully cooked.
3. In a large bowl, combine diced avocados, cherry tomatoes, red onion, and basil.
4. Slice the grilled salmon and add to the salad.
5. Drizzle with the remaining olive oil and balsamic vinegar. Toss gently to combine.
6. Season with salt and pepper to taste.
7. Serve immediately, enjoying the fresh and hearty flavors.

Nutritional: Calories: 450 kcal | Protein: 35 g | Carbohydrates: 12 g | Fat: 30 g | Fiber: 7 g | Sugar: 3 g

INGREDIENTS

- 4 swordfish steaks (6 ounces each)
- 2 tablespoons olive oil
- Salt and pepper to taste
- 1 mango, peeled and diced
- 1/2 red bell pepper, diced
- 1/4 cup red onion, finely chopped
- 1 jalapeño, seeded and minced (optional)
- Juice of 1 lime
- 1/4 cup fresh cilantro, chopped

58. Grilled Swordfish Steak with Mango Salsa and Cilantro

★★☆☆☆

🕐 10 Minutes   🍳🕐 0 Minutes   🍴 4 servings

INSTRUCTIONS

1. Preheat grill to medium-high heat.
2. Brush swordfish steaks with olive oil and season with salt and pepper.
3. Grill for about 5 minutes on each side or until the fish is opaque and flakes easily with a fork.
4. To make the mango salsa, combine mango, red bell pepper, red onion, jalapeño (if using), lime juice, and cilantro in a bowl. Mix well.
5. Serve the grilled swordfish topped with the fresh mango salsa.

Nutritional: Calories: 320 kcal | Protein: 28 g | Carbohydrates: 14 g | Fat: 16 g | Fiber: 2 g | Sugar: 10 g

59. Salmon Avocado and Tomato Salad

★★☆☆☆

🕐 10 Minutes   ♨🕐 25 Minutes   🍴 4 servings

INGREDIENTS

- 1 tablespoon olive oil
- 1 small onion, finely chopped
- 2 cloves garlic, minced
- 1 cup Arborio rice
- 1/2 cup white wine
- 4 cups seafood broth, heated
- 1 cup asparagus, trimmed and cut into 1-inch pieces
- 1 cup peas, fresh or frozen
- 1/2 pound mixed seafood (shrimp, scallops, and squid rings)
- Salt and pepper to taste
- Fresh parsley, chopped for garnish
- 1/4 cup grated Parmesan cheese (optional)

INSTRUCTIONS

1. Heat olive oil in a large skillet over medium heat. Add onion and garlic, sauté until soft.
2. Add Arborio rice and stir to coat with oil. Toast for about 2 minutes.
3. Pour in white wine and stir until mostly absorbed.
4. Add warm seafood broth one ladle at a time, stirring constantly until each addition is absorbed before adding more.
5. Halfway through, add asparagus and peas.
6. When the rice is nearly done and creamy, add the mixed seafood and cook until just done, about 3-4 minutes.
7. Season with salt and pepper. Stir in Parmesan cheese if using.
8. Garnish with fresh parsley and serve hot.

Nutritional: Calories: 420 kcal | Protein: 25 g | Carbohydrates: 53 g | Fat: 10 g | Fiber: 4 g | Sugar: 5 g

60. Grilled Sea Bass Slice on Spinach

★★☆☆☆

🕐 10 Minutes   ♨🕐 0 Minutes   🍴 4 servings

INGREDIENTS

- 4 sea bass slices (6 ounces each)
- 2 tablespoons olive oil
- Salt and pepper to taste
- 4 cups fresh spinach
- 1 garlic clove, minced
- Lemon wedges for serving

INSTRUCTIONS

1. Preheat grill to medium-high heat.
2. Brush sea bass slices with olive oil and season with salt and pepper.
3. Grill for about 4-5 minutes on each side or until the fish is opaque and flakes easily with a fork.
4. While the fish is grilling, heat a small amount of olive oil in a pan over medium heat. Add minced garlic and quickly sauté.
5. Add spinach to the pan and sauté until just wilted.
6. Serve the grilled sea bass over the sautéed spinach and squeeze lemon over the top before serving.

Nutritional: Calories: 290 kcal | Protein: 25 g | Carbohydrates: 2 g | Fat: 20 g | Fiber: 1 g | Sugar: 0 g

61. Seared Tuna Steak with Sesame Seeds, Soy Sauce, and Wasabi

★★★★★

🕐 10 Minutes   ♨🕐 5 Minutes   🍴 4 servings

INGREDIENTS

- 4 tuna steaks (6 ounces each)
- 2 tablespoons sesame oil
- 1/4 cup sesame seeds
- Salt and pepper to taste
- 4 tablespoons soy sauce
- 2 teaspoons wasabi paste
- 1 tablespoon fresh ginger, grated

INSTRUCTIONS

1. Heat sesame oil in a skillet over high heat.
2. Season the tuna steaks with salt and pepper, then coat each side with sesame seeds, pressing gently to adhere.
3. Sear the tuna steaks in the hot oil for about 1-2 minutes per side for medium-rare (adjust time if you prefer more or less doneness).
4. Remove from heat and slice thinly.
5. Mix soy sauce, wasabi, and grated ginger in a small bowl.
6. Serve the tuna steaks with the soy sauce mixture as a dipping sauce.

Nutritional: Calories: 350 kcal | Protein: 40 g | Carbohydrates: 4 g | Fat: 18 g | Fiber: 1 g | Sugar: 0 g

62. Grilled Salmon Fillet with Dill Sauce and Asparagus

★★★★★

🕐 10 Minutes   ♨🕐 0 Minutes   🍴 4 servings

INGREDIENTS

- 4 salmon fillets (6 ounces each)
- 2 tablespoons olive oil
- 1 pound asparagus, trimmed
- Salt and pepper to taste
- 1/2 cup Greek yogurt
- 1 tablespoon fresh dill, chopped
- 1 lemon, juiced
- Lemon wedges for serving

INSTRUCTIONS

1. Preheat grill to medium-high heat.
2. Brush salmon fillets and asparagus with olive oil; season with salt and pepper.
3. Grill the salmon, skin-side down, and asparagus for about 5 minutes per side, or until the salmon is cooked through and asparagus is tender.
4. In a small bowl, combine Greek yogurt, chopped dill, and lemon juice. Stir to combine.
5. Serve grilled salmon and asparagus with a dollop of dill sauce and lemon wedges on the side.

Nutritional: Calories: 300 kcal | Protein: 34 g | Carbohydrates: 5 g | Fat: 16 g | Fiber: 2 g | Sugar: 3 g

63. Grilled Shrimp Skewers with Lemon Wedges

★★★★★

🕐 10 Minutes   🍳🕐 5 Minutes   🍴 4 servings

INGREDIENTS

- 1 pound large shrimp, peeled and deveined
- 2 tablespoons olive oil
- Salt and pepper to taste
- 1 teaspoon paprika
- 1 lemon, cut into wedges

INSTRUCTIONS

1. Preheat the grill to high heat.
2. Thread the shrimp onto skewers.
3. Brush shrimp with olive oil and season with salt, pepper, and paprika.
4. Grill shrimp skewers for about 2-3 minutes per side, or until shrimp are opaque and cooked through.
5. Serve hot with lemon wedges for squeezing over the shrimp.

Nutritional: Calories: 180 kcal | Protein: 23 g | Carbohydrates: 2 g | Fat: 9 g | Fiber: 0 g | Sugar: 0 g

64. Grilled Prawns Served with Spicy Seafood Dipping Sauce

★★★★★

🕐 15 Minutes   🍳🕐 5 Minutes   🍴 4 servings

INGREDIENTS

- 1 pound prawns, peeled and deveined
- 2 tablespoons olive oil
- Salt and pepper to taste
- 1/4 cup ketchup
- 1 tablespoon hot sauce
- 1 tablespoon honey
- 1 garlic clove, minced
- Juice of 1 lime

INSTRUCTIONS

1. Preheat the grill to high heat.
2. Brush prawns with olive oil and season with salt and pepper.
3. Grill prawns for about 2 minutes per side, or until pink and cooked through.
4. In a small bowl, combine ketchup, hot sauce, honey, minced garlic, and lime juice to make the dipping sauce.
5. Serve the grilled prawns with the spicy seafood dipping sauce on the side.

Nutritional: Calories: 220 kcal | Protein: 24 g | Carbohydrates: 11 g | Fat: 9 g | Fiber: 0 g | Sugar: 9 g

MEAT

65. Chicken with Lemon Slices

 10 Minutes   25 Minutes   4 servings

INGREDIENTS

- 1 pound large shrimp, peeled and deveined
- 2 tablespoons olive oil
- Salt and pepper to taste
- 1 teaspoon paprika
- 1 lemon, cut into wedges

INSTRUCTIONS

1. Preheat the grill to high heat.
2. Thread the shrimp onto skewers.
3. Brush shrimp with olive oil and season with salt, pepper, and paprika.
4. Grill shrimp skewers for about 2-3 minutes per side, or until shrimp are opaque and cooked through.
5. Serve hot with lemon wedges for squeezing over the shrimp.

Nutritional: Calories: 220 kcal | Protein: 26 g | Carbohydrates: 5 g | Fat: 11 g | Fiber: 1 g | Sugar: 1 g

66. Lamb Curry with Potatoes and Carrots

 15 Minutes   120 Minutes   4 servings

INGREDIENTS

- 1 pound lamb, cut into cubes
- 2 tablespoons vegetable oil
- 1 onion, chopped
- 2 cloves garlic, minced
- 2 tablespoons curry powder
- 1 can (14 oz) coconut milk
- 2 potatoes, peeled and diced
- 2 carrots, peeled and sliced
- Salt and pepper to taste
- Fresh cilantro, for garnish

INSTRUCTIONS

1. Heat vegetable oil in a large pot over medium heat. Add onion and garlic, cook until softened.
2. Add lamb and curry powder, and brown the meat on all sides.
3. Pour in coconut milk and bring to a simmer.
4. Add potatoes and carrots, then cover and simmer for about 45 minutes, or until the meat is tender and the vegetables are cooked.
5. Season with salt and pepper.
6. Serve hot, garnished with fresh cilantro.

Nutritional: Calories: 220 kcal | Protein: 24 g | Carbohydrates: 11 g | Fat: 9 g | Fiber: 0 g | Sugar: 9 g

INGREDIENTS

- 16 asparagus spears, trimmed
- 8 slices bacon
- 1 tablespoon olive oil

67. Asparagus Wrapped with Fried Bacon

★★☆☆☆

10 Minutes   20 Minutes   4 servings

INSTRUCTIONS

1. Preheat the oven to 400°F (200°C).
2. Wrap each asparagus spear with half a slice of bacon. Secure with a toothpick if necessary.
3. Heat olive oil in a large oven-proof skillet over medium heat.
4. Add the bacon-wrapped asparagus and cook until the bacon starts to crisp, turning occasionally.
5. Transfer the skillet to the oven and roast for about 10 minutes, or until the asparagus is tender and the bacon is crispy.
6. Serve hot.

Nutritional: Calories: 200 kcal | Protein: 10 g | Carbohydrates: 2 g | Fat: 17 g | Fiber: 1 g | Sugar: 1 g

INGREDIENTS

- 4 steaks (such as ribeye or sirloin, about 6 ounces each)
- Salt and pepper to taste
- 1 tablespoon olive oil
- 1 cup fresh blueberries
- 2 tablespoons balsamic vinegar
- 1 tablespoon honey
- 1 teaspoon fresh rosemary, minced

68. Grilled Meat with Blueberry Sauce

★★★☆☆

15 Minutes   120 Minutes   4 servings

INSTRUCTIONS

1. Preheat grill to high heat.
2. Season steaks with salt and pepper and brush with olive oil.
3. Grill steaks to desired doneness, about 5-7 minutes per side for medium-rare.
4. While the steaks are grilling, combine blueberries, balsamic vinegar, honey, and rosemary in a small saucepan over medium heat.
5. Cook until blueberries have burst and the sauce has thickened, about 10 minutes.
6. Serve the grilled steaks drizzled with the blueberry sauce.

Nutritional: Calories: 420 kcal | Protein: 35 g | Carbohydrates: 12 g | Fat: 26 g | Fiber: 1 g | Sugar: 10 g

69. Scallops with Bacon

★★☆☆☆

🕐 10 Minutes   🍳🕐 20 Minutes   🍴 4 servings

INGREDIENTS

- 12 large sea scallops
- 6 slices bacon, cut in half
- Salt and pepper to taste
- 1 tablespoon olive oil
- Fresh parsley, chopped for garnish

INSTRUCTIONS

1. Wrap each scallop with a half slice of bacon and secure with a toothpick.
2. Season with salt and pepper.
3. Heat olive oil in a skillet over medium-high heat.
4. Add bacon-wrapped scallops and cook until bacon is crisp and scallops are opaque, about 3-4 minutes per side.
5. Serve garnished with fresh parsley.

Nutritional: Calories: 240 kcal | Protein: 15 g | Carbohydrates: 2 g | Fat: 18 g | Fiber: 0 g | Sugar: 0 g

70. Pork Knuckle Baked with Sauerkraut

★★★☆☆

🕐 20 Minutes   🍳🕐 240 Minutes   🍴 4 servings

INGREDIENTS

- 2 pork knuckles
- 2 tablespoons olive oil
- 1 onion, sliced
- 2 cups sauerkraut, drained
- 1 cup beer or apple cider
- Salt and pepper to taste
- 1 teaspoon caraway seeds (optional)

INSTRUCTIONS

1. Preheat the oven to 350°F (175°C).
2. Season pork knuckles with salt and pepper. Heat olive oil in a large ovenproof pot over high heat and brown the pork knuckles on all sides.
3. Remove pork knuckles and set aside. In the same pot, sauté onion until translucent.
4. Add sauerkraut, beer or cider, and caraway seeds if using. Stir to mix.
5. Return the pork knuckles to the pot, cover, and bake in the oven for about 2 hours, or until the meat is tender and falling off the bone.
6. Serve hot with sauerkraut.

Nutritional: Calories: 650 kcal | Protein: 48 g | Carbohydrates: 10 g | Fat: 45 g | Fiber: 3 g | Sugar: 3 g

71. Lamb Chops with Pesto Sauce

★★☆☆☆

🕐 10 Minutes   🍳🕐 20 Minutes   🍴 4 servings

INGREDIENTS

- 8 lamb chops
- Salt and pepper to taste
- 2 tablespoons olive oil
- 1/2 cup homemade or store-bought pesto sauce

INSTRUCTIONS

1. Season lamb chops with salt and pepper.
2. Heat olive oil in a large skillet over medium-high heat.
3. Add lamb chops and cook for about 3-4 minutes per side for medium-rare, or until they reach the desired level of doneness.
4. Remove from heat and let rest for a few minutes.
5. Serve lamb chops with a generous dollop of pesto sauce on top.

Nutritional: Calories: 400 kcal | Protein: 35 g | Carbohydrates: 2 g | Fat: 28 g | Fiber: 0.5 g | Sugar: 0.5 g

72. Meatballs with Tomato Sauce, Bell Pepper, Spring Onion, and Mint

★★★☆☆

🕐 20 Minutes   🍳🕐 240 Minutes   🍴 4 servings

INGREDIENTS

- 1 pound ground beef
- 1/4 cup breadcrumbs
- 1 egg
- 2 garlic cloves, minced
- 1/4 cup chopped fresh mint
- Salt and pepper to taste
- 1 tablespoon olive oil
- 1 bell pepper, diced
- 1/2 cup chopped spring onions
- 1 can (14 oz) crushed tomatoes
- 1 teaspoon sugar

INSTRUCTIONS

1. In a bowl, mix ground beef, breadcrumbs, egg, garlic, mint, salt, and pepper until well combined.
2. Form into small meatballs, about 1 inch in diameter.
3. Heat olive oil in a skillet over medium heat. Add meatballs and brown on all sides.
4. Remove meatballs and set aside. In the same skillet, add bell pepper and spring onions. Cook until soft.
5. Add crushed tomatoes and sugar, bring to a simmer.
6. Return meatballs to the skillet, cover, and simmer for 20 minutes.
7. Serve hot, garnished with extra chopped mint.

Nutritional: Calories: 380 kcal | Protein: 25 g | Carbohydrates: 15 g | Fat: 24 g | Fiber: 3 g | Sugar: 7 g

73. Chicken Fillet with Fresh Vegetable Salad of Tomatoes, Red Onions, and Lettuce

⏱ 10 Minutes   🍳⏱ 20 Minutes   🍴 4 servings

INGREDIENTS

- 4 chicken breast fillets
- Salt and pepper to taste
- 2 tablespoons olive oil
- 2 cups lettuce, chopped
- 1 cup cherry tomatoes, halved
- 1/2 red onion, thinly sliced
- 1/4 cup vinaigrette dressing

INSTRUCTIONS

1. Season chicken fillets with salt and pepper.
2. Heat olive oil in a skillet over medium heat. Cook chicken fillets until golden and cooked through, about 6-7 minutes per side.
3. Combine lettuce, cherry tomatoes, and red onion in a large salad bowl.
4. Slice the cooked chicken and add to the salad.
5. Drizzle with vinaigrette dressing and toss to combine.
6. Serve immediately.

Nutritional: Calories: 290 kcal | Protein: 28 g | Carbohydrates: 8 g | Fat: 16 g | Fiber: 2 g | Sugar: 4 g

74. Chicken Cacciatore

⏱ 20 Minutes   🍳⏱ 240 Minutes   🍴 4 servings

INGREDIENTS

- 4 chicken thighs, bone-in, skin-on
- Salt and pepper to taste
- 2 tablespoons olive oil
- 1 onion, chopped
- 2 garlic cloves, minced
- 1 bell pepper, sliced
- 1/2 cup white wine
- 1 can (14 oz) crushed tomatoes
- 1 teaspoon dried oregano
- 1 teaspoon dried basil
- Fresh parsley, chopped for garnish

INSTRUCTIONS

1. Season chicken thighs with salt and pepper.
2. Heat olive oil in a large skillet over medium-high heat. Add chicken and sear until golden brown on both sides, about 3-4 minutes per side. Remove chicken and set aside.
3. In the same skillet, add onion, garlic, and bell pepper. Sauté until softened, about 5 minutes.
4. Deglaze the pan with white wine, scraping up any browned bits from the bottom.
5. Stir in crushed tomatoes, oregano, and basil. Bring to a simmer.
6. Return the chicken to the skillet, cover, and simmer over low heat for 30 minutes, or until the chicken is cooked through.
7. Garnish with fresh parsley before serving.

Nutritional: Calories: 410 kcal | Protein: 25 g | Carbohydrates: 10 g | Fat: 28 g | Fiber: 2 g | Sugar: 4 g

75. Beef Carpaccio with Arugula and Sauce

⭐⭐☆☆☆

🕐 20 Minutes   ♨🕐 0 Minutes   🍴 4 servings

INGREDIENTS

- 1 pound beef tenderloin, thinly sliced
- 2 cups arugula
- 1/4 cup shaved Parmesan cheese
- 2 tablespoons olive oil
- 1 lemon, juiced
- Salt and pepper to taste
- 1 tablespoon capers, for garnish

INSTRUCTIONS

1. Arrange the thinly sliced beef tenderloin on a platter.
2. Top with arugula and shaved Parmesan cheese.
3. In a small bowl, whisk together olive oil and lemon juice. Season with salt and pepper.
4. Drizzle the dressing over the beef and arugula.
5. Garnish with capers.
6. Serve immediately, ensuring the beef remains fresh.

Nutritional: Calories: 320 kcal | Protein: 25 g | Carbohydrates: 2 g | Fat: 24 g | Fiber: 0.5 g | Sugar: 0.5 g

76. Grilled Barbecue Ribs with Sauce

⭐⭐⭐☆☆

🕐 15 Minutes   ♨🕐 120 Minutes   🍴 4 servings

INGREDIENTS

- 2 racks of pork ribs (about 2 pounds each)
- Salt and pepper to taste
- 1 cup barbecue sauce

INSTRUCTIONS

1. Preheat the oven to 275°F (135°C).
2. Season ribs with salt and pepper and brush with olive oil.
3. Wrap ribs tightly in aluminum foil and place on a baking sheet.
4. Bake in the preheated oven for about 1.5 hours or until tender.
5. Remove ribs from the oven and discard the foil. Increase oven temperature to 350°F (175°C).
6. Brush ribs with barbecue sauce and return to the oven, uncovered, for an additional 30 minutes.
7. Serve hot, slathered with more barbecue sauce if desired.

Nutritional: Calories: 600 kcal | Protein: 40 g | Carbohydrates: 20 g | Fat: 40 g | Fiber: 0 g | Sugar: 15 g

77. Grilled Steak and Pear Salad with Blue Cheese

★★★★★

🕐 15 Minutes   ♨🕐 10 Minutes   🍴 4 servings

INGREDIENTS

- 4 sirloin steaks (about 6 ounces each)
- Salt and pepper to taste
- 2 tablespoons olive oil
- 2 ripe pears, sliced
- 4 cups mixed salad greens
- 1/2 cup crumbled blue cheese
- 1/4 cup walnuts, toasted
- 3 tablespoons balsamic vinegar

INSTRUCTIONS

1. Preheat the grill to high heat.
2. Season steaks with salt and pepper and brush with 1 tablespoon olive oil.
3. Grill steaks for about 4-5 minutes per side for medium-rare, or until they reach the desired doneness.
4. Let steaks rest for a few minutes, then slice thinly.
5. In a large salad bowl, combine mixed greens, sliced pears, crumbled blue cheese, and toasted walnuts.
6. Whisk together balsamic vinegar and remaining olive oil, drizzle over the salad.
7. Top salad with sliced grilled steak and serve immediately.

Nutritional: Calories: 490 kcal | Protein: 36 g | Carbohydrates: 18 g | Fat: 32 g | Fiber: 3 g | Sugar: 12 g

76. Grilled Barbecue Ribs with Sauce

★★★★★

🕐 10 Minutes   ♨🕐 20 Minutes   🍴 4 servings

INGREDIENTS

- 4 chicken breasts, boneless and skinless
- Salt and pepper to taste
- 2 tablespoons olive oil
- 1 large onion, thinly sliced
- 2 tablespoons capers, rinsed
- 1 lemon, zest and juice
- Fresh parsley, chopped for garnish

INSTRUCTIONS

1. Season chicken breasts with salt and pepper.
2. Heat olive oil in a large skillet over medium-high heat.
3. Add chicken and cook until golden brown on both sides and cooked through, about 6-7 minutes per side.
4. Remove chicken from skillet and set aside.
5. In the same skillet, add onions and sauté until soft and caramelized, about 8 minutes.
6. Add capers and lemon zest, cook for an additional 2 minutes.
7. Return chicken to the skillet, squeeze over lemon juice, and heat through.
8. Garnish with fresh parsley before serving.

Nutritional: Calories: 300 kcal | Protein: 26 g | Carbohydrates: 6 g | Fat: 18 g | Fiber: 1 g | Sugar: 2 g

79. Duck Leg Steak with Orange Sauce

★★★★★

🕐 20 Minutes   🔥🕐 45 Minutes   🍴 4 servings

INGREDIENTS

- 4 duck legs
- Salt and pepper to taste
- 2 tablespoons olive oil
- 1 cup orange juice
- 2 tablespoons honey
- 1 tablespoon soy sauce
- 1 garlic clove, minced
- 1 teaspoon fresh ginger, grated

INSTRUCTIONS

1. Preheat the oven to 375°F (190°C).
2. Season duck legs with salt and pepper.
3. Heat olive oil in a skillet over medium-high heat. Sear duck legs until browned on all sides.
4. Transfer duck legs to a baking dish.
5. In a small saucepan, combine orange juice, honey, soy sauce, garlic, and ginger. Bring to a simmer and cook until slightly thickened, about 5 minutes.
6. Pour the orange sauce over the duck legs.
7. Bake in the preheated oven for 35-40 minutes, or until duck is tender and sauce is caramelized.
8. Serve duck legs with extra sauce drizzled over the top.

Nutritional: Calories: 600 kcal | Protein: 30 g | Carbohydrates: 20 g | Fat: 42 g | Fiber: 0 g | Sugar: 15 g

80. Roasted Beef with Mashed Potatoes

★★★★☆

🕐 20 Minutes   🔥🕐 90 Minutes   🍴 4 servings

INGREDIENTS

- 2 pounds beef roast
- 2 tablespoons olive oil
- Salt and pepper to taste
- 4 large potatoes, peeled and quartered
- 1/4 cup milk
- 2 tablespoons butter
- 1/4 cup sour cream
- Fresh chives, chopped for garnish

INSTRUCTIONS

1. Preheat oven to 350°F (175°C).
2. Rub the beef roast with olive oil, salt, and pepper.
3. Place in a roasting pan and roast in the preheated oven for about 1 hour 30 minutes, or until the internal temperature reaches 145°F (63°C) for medium rare.
4. Meanwhile, boil the potatoes in salted water until tender, about 20 minutes.
5. Drain potatoes and mash with milk, butter, and sour cream until smooth. Season with salt and pepper.
6. Slice the roasted beef and serve with the mashed potatoes. Garnish with chopped chives.

Nutritional: Calories: 300 kcal | Protein: 26 g | Carbohydrates: 6 g | Fat: 18 g | Fiber: 1 g | Sugar: 2 g

VEGAN

81. Chickpea and Vegetable Mix

★★★☆☆

🕐 10 Minutes   ♨🕐 20 Minutes   🍴 4 servings

INGREDIENTS

- 1 can (15 oz) chickpeas, drained and rinsed
- 2 tablespoons olive oil
- 1 red bell pepper, diced
- 1 zucchini, diced
- 1 yellow squash, diced
- 1 onion, diced
- 2 cloves garlic, minced
- 1 teaspoon ground cumin
- 1/2 teaspoon smoked paprika
- Salt and pepper to taste
- Fresh parsley, chopped for garnish

INSTRUCTIONS

1. Heat olive oil in a large skillet over medium heat.
2. Add onion and garlic, and sauté until translucent.
3. Add red bell pepper, zucchini, and yellow squash. Cook until the vegetables begin to soften, about 5-7 minutes.
4. Stir in chickpeas, cumin, and smoked paprika. Cook for another 5 minutes until everything is heated through and flavors meld.
5. Season with salt and pepper to taste.
6. Garnish with fresh parsley before serving.

Nutritional: Calories: 210 kcal | Protein: 7 g | Carbohydrates: 28 g | Fat: 9 g | Fiber: 7 g | Sugar: 7 g

82. Baked Zucchini with Mushrooms and Fresh Herbs

★★★☆☆

🕐 10 Minutes   ♨🕐 20 Minutes   🍴 4 servings

INGREDIENTS

- 4 medium zucchinis, sliced
- 1 cup mushrooms, sliced
- 2 tablespoons olive oil
- Salt and pepper to taste
- 1/2 cup grated Parmesan cheese (vegan)
- Fresh herbs (parsley, thyme, basil), chopped

INSTRUCTIONS

1. Preheat the oven to 200 °C (392 °F).
2. Arrange the zucchini and mushroom slices on a baking sheet.
3. Brush with olive oil and season with salt and pepper.
4. Sprinkle with grated Parmesan cheese.
5. Bake for 20 minutes, until the zucchini is tender and the cheese is melted and golden.
6. Garnish with chopped fresh herbs before serving.

Nutritional: Calories: 160 kcal | Protein: 8 g | Carbohydrates: 8 g | Fat: 11 g | Fiber: 2 g | Sugar: 5 g

INGREDIENTS

- 1 cup cooked quinoa
- 1 cup pumpkin puree
- 1/2 cup breadcrumbs
- 1/4 cup finely chopped onion
- 1 clove garlic, minced
- 1 teaspoon ground cumin
- Salt and pepper to taste
- 2 tablespoons olive oil
- Mixed greens for salad
- 1 tablespoon balsamic vinegar for dressing

83. Vegan Pumpkin and Quinoa Cutlets with Salad

★★★☆☆

20 Minutes   30 Minutes   4 servings

INSTRUCTIONS

1. In a large bowl, mix together the cooked quinoa, pumpkin puree, breadcrumbs, onion, garlic, cumin, salt, and pepper until well combined.
2. Shape the mixture into patties.
3. Heat olive oil in a skillet over medium heat. Fry the patties for about 4-5 minutes on each side, or until golden brown and crispy.
4. Serve the quinoa cutlets on a bed of mixed greens, drizzled with balsamic vinegar.

Nutritional: Calories: 270 kcal | Protein: 6 g | Carbohydrates: 33 g | Fat: 13 g | Fiber: 5 g | Sugar: 5 g

INGREDIENTS

- 1 cup quinoa
- 2 cups water
- 1/2 cucumber, diced
- 1 bell pepper, diced
- 1/4 cup chopped fresh parsley
- 1/4 cup chopped fresh mint
- 3 tablespoons olive oil
- Juice of 1 lemon
- Salt and pepper to taste

84. Quinoa Salad Garnished with Fresh Herbs

★★★☆☆

10 Minutes   20 Minutes   4 servings

INSTRUCTIONS

1. Rinse the quinoa under cold water until the water runs clear.
2. Bring water to a boil in a medium saucepan. Add quinoa, reduce heat to low, cover, and simmer for 15 minutes or until water is absorbed.
3. Let the quinoa cool, then fluff with a fork.
4. In a large bowl, combine the cooked quinoa, cucumber, bell pepper, parsley, and mint.
5. In a small bowl, whisk together olive oil, lemon juice, salt, and pepper.
6. Pour the dressing over the salad and toss to coat.
7. Serve chilled or at room temperature.

Nutritional: Calories: 240 kcal | Protein: 6 g | Carbohydrates: 28 g | Fat: 12 g | Fiber: 4 g | Sugar: 2 g

85. Eggplant Grilled with Tomato Sauce

★★★☆☆

🕐 10 Minutes   ⏲ 20 Minutes   🍴 4 servings

INSTRUCTIONS

1. Preheat the grill to medium-high heat.
2. Brush eggplant slices with olive oil and season with salt and pepper.
3. Grill eggplant slices for about 4-5 minutes on each side or until tender and grill marks appear.
4. Spoon tomato sauce over each slice and top with mozzarella cheese if using.
5. Close the grill lid and cook for an additional 5 minutes or until the cheese is melted and bubbly.
6. Garnish with fresh basil leaves before serving.

INGREDIENTS

- 2 large eggplants, sliced into 1/2-inch rounds
- Salt and pepper to taste
- 2 tablespoons olive oil
- 1 cup tomato sauce
- 1/2 cup shredded mozzarella cheese (optional for vegan)
- Fresh basil leaves for garnish

Nutritional: Calories: 180 kcal | Protein: 5 g | Carbohydrates: 20 g | Fat: 10 g | Fiber: 7 g | Sugar: 10 g

86. Vegan Hummus with Chickpeas

★★★☆☆

🕐 10 Minutes   ⏲ 0 Minutes   🍴 4 servings

INSTRUCTIONS

1. In a food processor, blend chickpeas, tahini, garlic, olive oil, and lemon juice until smooth.
2. Season with salt and pepper to taste.
3. Transfer to a serving bowl and create a shallow well in the center of the hummus.
4. Drizzle a little olive oil into the well and sprinkle paprika over the top for color.
5. Serve with fresh vegetables, pita bread, or as a spread on sandwiches.

INGREDIENTS

- 1 can (15 oz) chickpeas, drained and rinsed
- 1/4 cup tahini
- 2 cloves garlic, minced
- 2 tablespoons olive oil
- Juice of 1 lemon
- Salt and pepper to taste
- Paprika and olive oil for garnish

Nutritional: Calories: 260 kcal | Protein: 9 g | Carbohydrates: 20 g | Fat: 18 g | Fiber: 5 g | Sugar: 0 g

87. Spaghetti with Pesto and Vegan Parmesan Cheese

★★★☆☆

10 Minutes   10 Minutes   4 servings

INGREDIENTS

- 12 oz spaghetti
- 1 cup basil pesto (vegan)
- 1/4 cup vegan parmesan cheese, grated
- Salt and pepper to taste

INSTRUCTIONS

1. Cook spaghetti according to package instructions until al dente. Drain, reserving a little cooking water.
2. Return spaghetti to the pot and mix with basil pesto, adding a bit of reserved pasta water to help coat the spaghetti evenly.
3. Season with salt and pepper.
4. Serve hot, sprinkled with vegan parmesan cheese.

Nutritional: Calories: 410 kcal | Protein: 12 g | Carbohydrates: 56 g | Fat: 16 g | Fiber: 4 g | Sugar: 3 g

88. Asparagus Risotto with Lemon Zest

★★★★★

10 Minutes   25 Minutes   4 servings

INGREDIENTS

- 1 tablespoon olive oil
- 1 small onion, finely chopped
- 1 cup Arborio rice
- 1/2 cup white wine
- 3-4 cups vegetable broth, heated
- 1 bunch asparagus, trimmed and cut into 1-inch pieces
- Zest of 1 lemon
- Salt and pepper to taste
- 1/4 cup vegan parmesan cheese, grated (optional)

INSTRUCTIONS

1. Heat olive oil in a large skillet over medium heat. Add onion and sauté until translucent.
2. Add Arborio rice and stir to coat with oil. Cook for 1-2 minutes until the rice becomes slightly translucent.
3. Pour in white wine and stir until mostly absorbed.
4. Add heated vegetable broth one ladle at a time, stirring constantly until each ladle is absorbed before adding the next. Continue until rice is creamy and just tender.
5. Midway through cooking, add asparagus.
6. Once risotto is done, stir in lemon zest and season with salt and pepper.
7. Serve hot, sprinkled with vegan parmesan cheese if desired.

Nutritional: Calories: 340 kcal | Protein: 8 g | Carbohydrates: 52 g | Fat: 9 g | Fiber: 3 g | Sugar: 3 g

INGREDIENTS

- 4 large bell peppers (red, yellow, or orange)
- 1 cup cooked quinoa
- 1 can (15 oz) chickpeas, drained and rinsed
- 1 cup diced tomatoes
- 1/2 cup chopped red onion
- 1/4 cup chopped fresh parsley
- 1/4 cup chopped fresh mint
- 1/4 cup chopped kalamata olives
- 1/4 cup pine nuts
- 2 tablespoons olive oil
- 2 tablespoons lemon juice
- 1 teaspoon ground cumin
- Salt and pepper to taste

89. Mediterranean Stuffed Peppers

★★★★★

10 Minutes   15 Minutes   4 servings

INSTRUCTIONS

1. Preheat the oven: Preheat your oven to 200 degrees Celsius (400 degrees Fahrenheit).
2. Prepare the peppers: Cut the tops off the bell peppers and remove the seeds and membranes. If necessary, trim the bottoms slightly to make them stand upright.
3. Make the filling: In a large bowl, combine the cooked quinoa, chickpeas, diced tomatoes, red onion, parsley, mint, kalamata olives, and pine nuts. Add the olive oil, lemon juice, ground cumin, salt, and pepper. Mix well to combine all ingredients.
4. Stuff the peppers: Fill each bell pepper with the quinoa mixture, packing it in tightly.
5. Bake: Place the stuffed peppers in a baking dish. Cover the dish with aluminum foil and bake in the preheated oven for 20 minutes. Remove the foil and bake for an additional 10 minutes, until the peppers are tender and slightly charred on the edges.
6. Serve: Remove from the oven and let cool slightly before serving. Garnish with extra parsley or mint if desired.

Nutritional: Calories: Calories: 280 kcal | Protein: 7 g | Carbs: 35 g | Fat: 12 g | Fiber: 9 g | Sugar: 8 g

DESSERT

90. Lemon Cheesecake

★★★★★

🕐 20 Minutes    50 Minutes   🍴 4 servings

INGREDIENTS

- 1 1/2 cups graham cracker crumbs
- 1/3 cup unsalted butter, melted
- 2 tablespoons sugar
- 3 packages (8 oz each) cream cheese, softened
- 1 cup sugar
- 3 large eggs
- Zest and juice of 2 lemons
- 1 teaspoon vanilla extract

INSTRUCTIONS

1. Preheat oven to 350°F (175°C).
2. Combine graham cracker crumbs, melted butter, and 2 tablespoons sugar. Press into the bottom of a 9-inch springform pan.
3. In a large mixing bowl, beat cream cheese and 1 cup sugar until smooth.
4. Add eggs, one at a time, beating well after each addition.
5. Mix in lemon zest, lemon juice, and vanilla extract until well combined.
6. Pour filling over the crust in the springform pan.
7. Bake for 45-50 minutes or until the center is set.
8. Allow to cool, then refrigerate for at least 4 hours before serving.

Nutritional: Calories: 480 kcal | Protein: 8 g | Carbohydrates: 40 g | Fat: 34 g | Fiber: 0 g | Sugar: 30 g

91. Cheesecake with Raspberry Coulis and Mint

★★★★★

20 Minutes   60 Minutes   8 servings

INGREDIENTS

- For the Cheesecake:
- 1 1/2 cups graham cracker crumbs
- 1/3 cup unsalted butter, melted
- 2 tablespoons sugar
- 3 packages (8 oz each) cream cheese, softened
- 1 cup sugar
- 3 large eggs
- 1 teaspoon vanilla extract
- For the Raspberry Coulis:
- 2 cups fresh raspberries
- 1/4 cup sugar
- Juice of 1 lemon
- For Garnish:
- Fresh mint leaves
- Additional raspberries

INSTRUCTIONS

1. Crust: Preheat oven to 350°F (175°C). Mix graham cracker crumbs, melted butter, and 2 tablespoons sugar together. Press into the bottom of a 9-inch springform pan. Set aside.
2. Filling: In a large bowl, beat cream cheese and 1 cup sugar until smooth. Add eggs, one at a time, mixing well after each addition. Stir in vanilla extract. Pour over the crust in the springform pan.
3. Bake: Bake in preheated oven for 45-50 minutes or until the center is almost set. Allow to cool, then refrigerate for at least 4 hours.
4. Raspberry Coulis: Combine raspberries, 1/4 cup sugar, and lemon juice in a saucepan over medium heat. Cook until berries break down, about 10 minutes. Strain through a fine-mesh sieve to remove seeds.
5. Serve: Drizzle raspberry coulis over each slice of cheesecake. Garnish with fresh mint leaves and additional raspberries.

Nutritional: Calories: 550 kcal | Protein: 9 g | Carbohydrates: 50 g | Fat: 35 g | Fiber: 2 g | Sugar: 38 g

92. Fresh and Colorful Mixed Berry Fruit Salad

★★★★★

10 Minutes   0 Minutes   6 servings

INGREDIENTS

- 1 cup strawberries, hulled and halved
- 1 cup blueberries
- 1 cup raspberries
- 1 cup blackberries
- 2 tablespoons honey
- Juice of 1 lime
- Fresh mint leaves for garnish

INSTRUCTIONS

1. In a large bowl, combine all the berries gently.
2. Drizzle honey and lime juice over the berries, and toss to coat evenly.
3. Chill in the refrigerator until ready to serve.
4. Garnish with fresh mint leaves before serving.

Nutritional: Calories: 90 kcal | Protein: 1 g | Carbohydrates: 22 g | Fat: 0.5 g | Fiber: 4 g | Sugar: 16 g

93. Caramel Cake with Hazelnuts and Mousse on White

⭐⭐⭐⭐⭐

30 Minutes   **60 Minutes**   **8 servings**

INGREDIENTS

- **For the Cake:**
- 1/2 cup unsalted butter, softened
- 1 cup sugar
- 2 eggs
- 1 teaspoon vanilla extract
- 2 cups all-purpose flour
- 1 teaspoon baking powder
- 1/2 teaspoon salt
- 1 cup milk
- **For the Caramel Mousse:**
- 1 cup sugar
- 1/4 cup water
- 1 cup heavy cream
- 1/2 teaspoon vanilla extract
- 1/2 cup chopped hazelnuts, toasted

INSTRUCTIONS

1. Cake:Preheat oven to 350°F (175°C). Grease and flour a 9-inch round cake pan.Cream butter and sugar until light and fluffy. Add eggs and vanilla, beating well.Combine flour, baking powder, and salt; add to creamed mixture alternately with milk. Pour into prepared pan and bake for 30-35 minutes.
2. Caramel Mousse: In a saucepan, combine sugar and water. Heat until sugar dissolves and turns a golden caramel color. Carefully stir in heavy cream (mixture will bubble) and vanilla. Cool to room temperature. Whip the cooled caramel until fluffy.
3. Assemble: Once the cake is cooled, top with caramel mousse and sprinkle with toasted hazelnuts.
4. Chill: Refrigerate for at least 2 hours before serving.

Nutritional: Calories: 510 kcal | Protein: 7 g | Carbohydrates: 70 g | Fat: 23 g | Fiber: 2 g | Sugar: 48 g

94. Catalan Cream

⭐⭐⭐⭐⭐

20 Minutes   **50 Minutes**   **4 servings**

INGREDIENTS

- 2 cups heavy cream
- 1 cinnamon stick
- Peel of 1 lemon
- 1/2 cup sugar, plus extra for topping
- 6 egg yolks
- 1 teaspoon vanilla extract

INSTRUCTIONS

1. In a saucepan, combine heavy cream, cinnamon stick, and lemon peel. Bring to a simmer over medium heat, then remove from heat and let infuse for 10 minutes.
2. In a bowl, whisk together egg yolks and 1/2 cup sugar until pale and thick. Gradually whisk in the warm cream (strain to remove cinnamon and lemon peel).
3. Return the mixture to the saucepan and cook over low heat, stirring constantly, until the mixture thickens enough to coat the back of a spoon.
4. Remove from heat, stir in vanilla extract, and pour into four ramekins.
5. Chill in the refrigerator for at least 2 hours.
6. Before serving, sprinkle each ramekin with a thin layer of sugar and use a kitchen torch to caramelize the top. Serve immediately after caramelizing.

Nutritional: Calories: 570 kcal | Protein: 6 g | Carbohydrates: 40 g | Fat: 44 g | Fiber: 0 g | Sugar: 37 g

INGREDIENTS

- 6 egg yolks
- 3/4 cup sugar
- 1 cup mascarpone cheese
- 1 1/2 cups strong coffee, cooled
- 2 tablespoons dark rum or coffee liqueur
- 2 cups ladyfingers
- Cocoa powder for dusting

95. Tiramisu

★★★★★

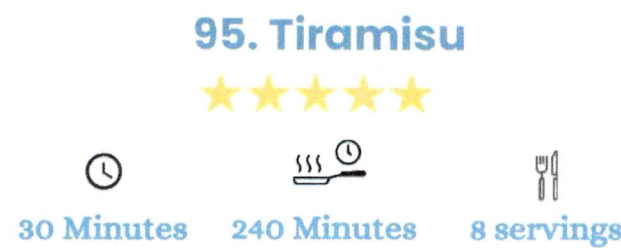

30 Minutes   240 Minutes   8 servings

INSTRUCTIONS

1. In a large bowl, beat egg yolks and sugar until thick and pale. Fold in mascarpone until smooth.
2. Mix the coffee and rum in a shallow dish. Briefly dip each ladyfinger into the coffee mixture, making sure they are not soggy.
3. Arrange half of the soaked ladyfingers in the bottom of an 8x8 inch dish.
4. Spread half of the mascarpone mixture over the ladyfingers.
5. Repeat with another layer of soaked ladyfingers and mascarpone mixture.
6. Cover and chill in the refrigerator for at least 4 hours.
7. Dust with cocoa powder before serving.

Nutritional: Calories: 390 kcal | Protein: 6 g | Carbohydrates: 33 g | Fat: 26 g | Fiber: 0 g | Sugar: 22 g

INGREDIENTS

- 1 cup butter, softened
- 1 cup brown sugar
- 1/2 cup white sugar
- 2 eggs
- 1 teaspoon vanilla extract
- 1 1/2 cups all-purpose flour
- 1 teaspoon baking soda
- 1/2 teaspoon salt
- 3 cups rolled oats
- 1 cup raisins

96. Oatmeal Cookies

★★★★☆

15 Minutes   12 Minutes   24 servings

INSTRUCTIONS

1. Preheat oven to 350°F (175°C).
2. In a large bowl, cream together butter, brown sugar, and white sugar until smooth.
3. Beat in eggs one at a time, then stir in vanilla.
4. Combine flour, baking soda, and salt; stir into the creamed mixture until just blended.
5. Mix in oats and raisins.
6. Drop by heaping spoonfuls onto ungreased baking sheets.
7. Bake for 12 minutes in the preheated oven, or until golden brown. Allow cookies to cool on baking sheet for 5 minutes before transferring to a wire rack to cool completely.

Nutritional: Calories: 190 kcal | Protein: 3 g | Carbohydrates: 30 g | Fat: 7 g | Fiber: 2 g | Sugar: 16 g

INGREDIENTS

- For the crust:
- 2 1/2 cups all-purpose flour
- 1 teaspoon salt
- 1 teaspoon sugar
- 1 cup unsalted butter, chilled and diced
- 1/4-1/2 cup ice water
- For the filling:
- 6 cups sliced peeled apples (about 6 medium)
- 3/4 cup sugar
- 2 tablespoons all-purpose flour
- 1 teaspoon ground cinnamon
- 1/4 teaspoon ground nutmeg
- 2 tablespoons unsalted butter
- 1 egg yolk, beaten with 1 tablespoon water (for glaze)

97. Apple Pie

★★★★★

🕐 30 Minutes   ♨️🕐 45 Minutes   🍴 8 servings

INSTRUCTIONS

1. Prepare the crust: In a large bowl, mix flour, salt, and sugar. Add butter and use a pastry cutter to blend until the mixture resembles coarse crumbs. Gradually add ice water, stirring until the dough holds together without being wet or sticky. Split dough into two halves, form into balls, and flatten into disks. Wrap in plastic and refrigerate for at least 1 hour.
2. Prepare the filling: In a large bowl, toss apples with sugar, flour, cinnamon, and nutmeg until coated.
3. Assemble the pie: Roll out one disk of dough on a floured surface to fit a 9-inch pie plate. Place crust in pie plate. Fill with apple mixture, and dot with pieces of butter. Roll out the second disk of dough, place over the filling, and trim, seal, and flute the edges. Cut slits in the top to allow steam to escape. Brush the crust with the egg yolk glaze.
4. Bake: Preheat oven to 375°F (190°C). Bake in the preheated oven for about 45 minutes, or until the crust is golden brown and the filling is bubbly. Cool on a wire rack before serving.

Nutritional: Calories: 510 kcal | Protein: 5 g | Carbohydrates: 65 g | Fat: 26 g | Fiber: 3 g | Sugar: 35 g

INGREDIENTS

- 2 cups water
- 1 cup sugar
- 1 cup fresh lemon juice (about 4-5 lemons)
- 1 tablespoon lemon zest
- 1/4 cup fresh basil leaves, finely chopped

98. Lemon and Basil Sorbet

★★★★☆

🕐 10 Minutes   ♨️🕐 5 Minutes   🍴 6 servings

INSTRUCTIONS

1. In a medium saucepan, combine water and sugar. Bring to a boil, stirring until sugar dissolves completely.
2. Remove from heat and add lemon juice, lemon zest, and chopped basil.
3. Allow the mixture to cool to room temperature, then strain to remove solids.
4. Pour into an ice cream maker and freeze according to the manufacturer's instructions.
5. Transfer the sorbet to a container and freeze until firm, about 2-3 hours.
6. Serve in chilled bowls.

Nutritional: Calories: 190 kcal | Protein: 3 g | Carbohydrates: 30 g | Fat: 7 g | Fiber: 2 g | Sugar: 16 g

99. Vanilla Ice Cream Scoops with Caramel Syrup Frosting

★★★☆☆

🕐 15 Minutes   ♨🕐 0 Minutes   🍴 8 servings

INGREDIENTS

- 1 quart vanilla ice cream
- 1/2 cup caramel syrup
- Optional toppings: chopped nuts, chocolate shavings, or whipped cream

INSTRUCTIONS

1. Scoop vanilla ice cream into serving bowls.
2. Drizzle each serving with caramel syrup.
3. Add optional toppings such as chopped nuts, chocolate shavings, or whipped cream if desired.
4. Serve immediately.

Nutritional: Calories: 270 kcal | Protein: 4 g | Carbohydrates: 37 g | Fat: 12 g | Fiber: 1 g | Sugar: 30 g

100. Chocolate Cake with Almonds and Walnuts

★★★★★

🕐 20 Minutes   ♨🕐 35 Minutes   🍴 8 servings

INSTRUCTIONS

1. Preheat the oven to 175 degrees Celsius (350 degrees Fahrenheit). Grease and flour a 9-inch round cake pan.
2. Mix Dry Ingredients: In a large bowl, sift together the flour, granulated sugar, cocoa powder, baking powder, baking soda, and salt.
3. Combine Wet Ingredients: In another bowl, whisk together the vegetable oil, eggs, vanilla extract, and buttermilk until well combined.
4. Combine Wet and Dry Ingredients: Gradually add the wet ingredients to the dry ingredients, mixing until just combined. Stir in the hot water until the batter is smooth.
5. Add Nuts: Fold in the chopped almonds and walnuts, ensuring they are evenly distributed throughout the batter.
6. Bake the Cake: Pour the batter into the prepared cake pan. Bake in the preheated oven for 35 minutes, or until a toothpick inserted into the center of the cake comes out clean.
7. Cool and Serve: Allow the cake to cool in the pan for 10 minutes before transferring it to a wire rack to cool completely. Dust with powdered sugar if desired before serving.

INGREDIENTS

- 1 cup all-purpose flour
- 1 cup granulated sugar
- 1/2 cup unsweetened cocoa powder
- 1 teaspoon baking powder
- 1/2 teaspoon baking soda
- 1/2 teaspoon salt
- 1/2 cup vegetable oil
- 2 large eggs
- 1 teaspoon vanilla extract
- 1/2 cup buttermilk
- 1/2 cup hot water
- 1/2 cup chopped almonds
- 1/2 cup chopped walnuts
- 1/4 cup powdered sugar for dusting (optional)

Nutritional: Calories: 350 kcal | Protein: 5 g | Carbs: 45 g | Fat: 18 g | Fiber: 3 g | Sugar: 27 g

28 -Day Meal Plan

Day	Breakfast	Lunch	Dinner	Snacks
1	3. Shakshuka in a Frying Pan	27. Pasta with Basil Pesto and Cherry Tomatoes	74. Chicken Cacciatore	97. Apple Pie
2	1. Toast with Guacamole and Fried Egg Yolk	19. Mediterranean Chickpea Salad with Feta and Olives	55. Grilled Salmon Fillet with Lemon and Dill Garnish	90. Lemon Cheesecake
3	5. Lemon Muffin	22. Quinoa Tabbouleh with Cherry Tomatoes	65. Chicken with Lemon Slices	96. Oatmeal Cookies
4	2. Stacked Pancakes with Berries	16. Asparagus Lemon Risotto with Parmesan	43. Octopus Salad with Tomatoes and Parsley	98. Lemon and Basil Sorbet
5	9. Smoked Salmon Avocado Toast	25. Quinoa and Chickpea Salad with Lemon Tahini Dressing	67. Asparagus Wrapped with Fried Bacon	95. Tiramisu
6	6. Spinach and Ricotta Omelette	21. Haricot Beans in Tomato Sauce	47. Stir-Fried Mixed Vegetables with Shrimp	91. Cheesecake with Raspberry Coulis and Mint
7	8. Oatmeal Topped with Sliced Bananas and Nuts	24. Roasted Garlic Hummus Drizzled with Olive Oil	66. Lamb Curry with Potatoes and Carrots	94. Catalan Cream
8	4. Scrambled Eggs with Vegetables and Gluten-Free Toast	18. Savory Vegan Mushroom Risotto with Arborio Rice and Thyme	49. Grilled Fish with Roasted Potatoes and Vegetables	99. Vanilla Ice Cream Scoops with Caramel Syrup Frosting
9	10. Oat Bowl with Crunchy Almonds and Sweet Honey	28. Pasta with Garlic Shrimp Scampi	63. Grilled Shrimp Skewers with Lemon Wedges	92. Fresh and Colorful Mixed Berry Fruit Salad
10	11. Colorful Fresh Mixed Berry Fruit Salad	17. Mediterranean Farro Salad with Olives and Tomatoes	48. Pike Perch Fillet with Grilled Zucchini and White Sauce	100. Chocolate Cake with Almonds and Walnuts

11	7. Oatmeal Served with Yogurt and Fresh Fruit	23. Lentil Soup with Carrots, Celery, and Spinach	68. Grilled Meat with Blueberry Sauce	93. Caramel Cake with Hazelnuts and Mousse on White
12	12. Creamy Vegan Asparagus Risotto with Lemon Zest	20. Chickpea Salad with Cucumbers, Tomatoes, and Red Onions	58. Grilled Swordfish Steak with Mango Salsa and Cilantro	90. Lemon Cheesecake
13	15. Oat Banana Pancake with Yogurt and Nuts	30. Roasted Peppers with Garlic, Basil, and Tomato	72. Meatballs with Tomato Sauce, Bell Pepper, Spring Onion, and Mint	96. Oatmeal Cookies
14	13. Date-Goat Cheese Crostini	26. Zucchini Noodles with Flavorful Marinara Sauce and Vegan Parmesan	71. Lamb Chops with Pesto Sauce	98. Lemon and Basil Sorbet
15	14. Greek Yogurt and Spiced Apples	29. Grilled Zucchini and Eggplant	70. Pork Knuckle Baked with Sauerkraut	95. Tiramisu
16	1. Toast with Guacamole and Fried Egg Yolk	19. Mediterranean Chickpea Salad with Feta and Olives	45. Grilled Shrimp and Pineapple Skewers with Sweet Chili Glaze	91. Cheesecake with Raspberry Coulis and Mint
17	5. Lemon Muffin	22. Quinoa Tabbouleh with Cherry Tomatoes	76. Grilled Barbecue Ribs with Sauce	94. Catalan Cream
18	2. Stacked Pancakes with Berries	16. Asparagus Lemon Risotto with Parmesan	54. Grilled Striped Bass with Lemon and Herb	99. Vanilla Ice Cream Scoops with Caramel Syrup Frosting
19	9. Smoked Salmon Avocado Toast	25. Quinoa and Chickpea Salad with Lemon Tahini Dressing	79. Duck Leg Steak with Orange Sauce	92. Fresh and Colorful Mixed Berry Fruit Salad
20	6. Spinach and Ricotta Omelette	21. Haricot Beans in Tomato Sauce	69. Scallops with Bacon	100. Chocolate Cake with Almonds and Walnuts
21	8. Oatmeal Topped with Sliced Bananas and Nuts	24. Roasted Garlic Hummus Drizzled with Olive Oil	74. Chicken Cacciatore	97. Apple Pie

22	4. Scrambled Eggs with Vegetables and Gluten-Free Toast	18. Savory Vegan Mushroom Risotto with Arborio Rice and Thyme	51. Seafood Pasta Paella	93. Caramel Cake with Hazelnuts and Mousse on White
23	10. Oat Bowl with Crunchy Almonds and Sweet Honey	28. Pasta with Garlic Shrimp Scampi	80. Roasted Beef with Mashed Potatoes	90. Lemon Cheesecake
24	11. Colorful Fresh Mixed Berry Fruit Salad	17. Mediterranean Farro Salad with Olives and Tomatoes	78. Grilled Sea Bass Slice on Spinach	96. Oatmeal Cookies
25	7. Oatmeal Served with Yogurt and Fresh Fruit	23. Lentil Soup with Carrots, Celery, and Spinach	60. Grilled Sea Bass Slice on Spinach	98. Lemon and Basil Sorbet
26	12. Creamy Vegan Asparagus Risotto with Lemon Zest	20. Chickpea Salad with Cucumbers, Tomatoes, and Red Onions	73. Chicken Fillet with Fresh Vegetable Salad of Tomatoes, Red Onions, and Lettuce	95. Tiramisu
27	15. Oat Banana Pancake with Yogurt and Nuts	30. Roasted Peppers with Garlic, Basil, and Tomato	77. Grilled Steak and Pear Salad with Blue - Cheese	91. Cheesecake with Raspberry Coulis and Mint
28	13. Date-Goat Cheese Crostini	26. Zucchini Noodles with Flavorful Marinara Sauce and Vegan Parmesan	75. Beef Carpaccio with Arugula and Sauce	94. Catalan Cream

I kindly and wholeheartedly ask that if you enjoyed the work, please leave a review.

Your Exclusive Bonuses:

- 7 Secrets for Success with the Mediterranean Diet: Discover the secrets to getting the most out of your Mediterranean diet and enhancing your health.

- Video Recipes with Step-by-Step Explanations: Access exclusive video recipes that will guide you through the preparation of dishes, making everything even easier and more enjoyable.

Printed in Great Britain
by Amazon

56191884R00044